To

Mr Theodore G. Joslin and Wife:—

The author hopes you may find
pleasure in perusing these pages
and that you will come to the
Oregon Country and acquaint your
friends with it wonderful beauty.
We want you to enjoy the
Highway which men built as a frame
to the beautiful picture which God
created, and which is now paved like
a city street from the City of Portland
through the Gorge of the Columbia
into the heart of the Cascade
Range.

Samuel C. Lancaster
Portland Oregon
September 21st
1916

Foreword

I've traveled the old Columbia River highway on numerous occasions down through the years. Every time I do it I am blown away by its beauty. It's like time traveling! Woody Guthrie drove on this road, writing promotional songs for the Bonneville Power Administration. He penned such magnificent ballads as "Grand Coulee Dam," "Hard Travelin'," and "Roll On, Columbia." The year was 1941, and inspired by the landscape Woody composed 26 songs in one month's time.

I feel his spirit—looking upriver from the Vista House at Crown Point. At night, a crown of lights can be seen from the freeway below. The mighty monolith Beacon Rock beckons in the distance. Lewis and Clark wrote about it in their journals, as they headed downstream toward the Pacific Ocean. Rooster Rock, with a more phallic moniker in native legend, stands out along the sandy beach. Oregon Trail pioneers took note of these stone monuments and wonderful waterfalls as they approached the end of their journey from St. Louis. Their Conestoga wagons were being floated on flat boats, and they had to portage at the Cascade rapids. Later, steamboats and a little railroad, "The Oregon Pony," helped out.

It was a hellish and treacherous journey down the untamed waters before the Barlow Road was established in 1848. Past Celilo Falls, with its 12,000 years of native history, now underwater behind The Dalles Dam. At Cascade Locks, a modern "Bridge of the Gods" has been engineered. The name refers to perhaps the greatest Indian legend of the Columbia. Telling how the two brothers Wy'east (Mt. Hood) and Pahtoe (Mt. Adams) got into a volcanic spitting match over the witch Loo-wit (Mt. St. Helens). In anger, the Great Spirit collapsed the volcanic bridge that the tribes had used from time immemorial. Lewis and Clark found "drowned trees in the river," and modern-day geologists have tested their age, surmising a massive landslide that blocked the Columbia some 700 years ago and confirming native oral tradition.

Yes, this river passage through the Cascades, stretching from Troutdale on the Sandy River to The Dalles, has many tales to tell, including its own. The book you are now eagerly perusing went through three editions—the last one in 1926. It is a gorgeous volume with colored plates of a bygone era, filled with curious facts, diary entries, and personal reminiscences by one of the most esteemed highway engineers of his era. He was a booster and a boomer for good roads and the natural wonders that God placed here, especially in the Pacific Northwest.

Samuel C. Lancaster was a friend of the poets and artists. I know that from firsthand discovery. As a Portland poet and a book scout, I encountered two volumes from Mr. Lancaster's personal library. One inscribed to him by the crippled seamstress poet, Hazel Hall, and the other by Oregon poet laureate Ethel Romig Fuller with a Lancaster photo of the poet standing by her gingko tree. Hall's *Curtains* was particularly poignant because Lancaster, who'd been incapacitated by typhoid and infantile paralysis, gave her a week's hospitality at his place in the gorge in September of 1922. The engineer had empathy for someone who couldn't walk. His own 18-month ordeal is described on page 159.

(Continued on page 148).

COLUMBIA RIVER GORGE FROM CHANTICLEER—CROWN POINT ON THE RIGHT.

(Color photograph made September, 1914, just after grading had been completed around the top of the rock.)

The broad highway encircles the top of this great rock, which stands sheer seven hundred twenty-five feet above the River. Table Mountain on the left is three thousand four hundred twenty feet in elevation. From Crown Point the eye looks through the Cascade Mountain Range, a distance of thirty-five miles to the eastward, and almost as far in the direction of the setting sun, across the gleaming waters of the ever broadening stream.

The Columbia River is peerless. Its grandeur speaks to men, and tells of Him who gathered the waters together into one place, and lifted up the mountains.

The Columbia

America's Great Highway

through the

Cascade Mountains

to the Sea

BY

SAMUEL CHRISTOPHER LANCASTER

With twenty-six color plates and
other illustrations; twenty-one of them, by
the new process of color photography, first photographed
on glass direct from nature, and afterward
reproduced by the four color process.

4880 Lower Valley Road, Atglen, PA 19310 USA

This book is based upon the second edition, published in 1916, though additional images from the third edition in 1926 have been included. They are:

Library of Congress Cataloging-in-Publication
Data

Lancaster, Samuel Christopher.
    The Columbia, America's great highway through
the Cascade Mountains to the sea / by Samuel Christopher Lancaster.
       p. cm.
    Originally published: Portland, Or. : S.C.
Lancaster, 1915.
    ISB N 0-7643-2003-3 (pbk.)
1. Columbia River--Pictorial works. 2. Cascade
Range--Pictorial works. I. Title.
F853 .L242. 2004
979.7'04'40222--dc22
        2003024270
Copyright © 2004 by Schiffer Publishing, Ltd.

Front layout by "Sue"
Type set in Aldine 721 BT

ISBN: 0-7643-2003-3
Printed in China

Published by Schiffer Publishing Ltd.
4880 Lower Valley Road
Atglen, PA 19310
Phone: (610) 593-1777; Fax: (610) 593-2002
E-mail: info@schifferbooks.com

Please visit our web site catalog at
www.schifferbooks.com
We are always looking for people to write books on new and related subjects. If you have an idea for a book please contact us at the above address.

This book may be purchased from the publisher.
Include $3.95 for shipping.
Please try your bookstore first.
You may write for a free catalog.

In Europe, Schiffer books are distributed by
Bushwood Books
6 Marksbury Ave.
Kew Gardens
Surrey TW9 4JF England
Phone: 44 (0) 20 8392-8585; Fax: 44 (0) 20 8392-9876
E-mail: info@bushwoodbooks.co.uk
Free postage in the U.K., Europe;
air mail at cost.

Samuel Hill
ROAD BUILDER

G.F. Holman

Who loves this country and brought me to it.
Who showed me the German Rhine and Continental Europe.
Whose kindness made it possible for me to have a part in
planning and constructing this great highway

There is a time, and place for every man to act his part
in life's drama and to build according to his ideals

God shaped these great mountains round about us, and
lifted up those mighty domes into a region of perpetual snow

He fashioned the Gorge of the Columbia, fixed the course
of the broad river, and caused the crystal streams both small and
great, to leap down from the crags and sing their never ending
songs of joy.

Then He planted a garden, men came and built a
beautiful city close by this wonderland. To some He
gave great wealth — to every man his talent — and when
the time had come for men to break down the mountain barriers,
construct a great highway of commerce, and utilize the
beautiful, which is "as useful as the useful", He set them
to the task and gave to each his place.

I am thankful to God for His goodness in permitting
me to have a part in building this broad thoroughfare as a
frame to the beautiful picture which He created.

— Samuel Christopher Lancaster —
Highway Engineer
1915

COLUMBIA

RHINE

Oldest of living things; these gray old trunks lift
their mossy boughs into the heavens. They speak to
us of by-gone centuries and the silent work of God.

PREFACE

While engaged as Consulting Engineer in fixing the location and directing the construction of the Columbia River Highway from Portland east through the Cascade Range in Multnomah County, Oregon, I studied the landscape with much care and became acquainted with its formation and its geology.

I was profoundly impressed by its majestic beauty and marveled at the creative power of God, who made it all.

The everchanging lights and shadows from morning until night, made pictures rare and beautiful, which always charmed me, and I wondered if it were possible for some of them to be preserved by the new process of color photography. This proved to be entirely practical, and with the assistance of three friends, Mr. Frank I. Jones, Mr. Henry Berger, Jr., and Dr. N. L. Smith, we were able to accomplish this. I am greatly indebted to these gentlemen for their assistance in this work, which required many days and nights of tireless labor.

While going back and forth over the Columbia River Highway during its construction I carried my camera in a rain-proof bag in all kinds of weather, that I might be ready when God painted the pictures.

As I climbed about the steep slopes of the mountains, where in places it was necessary to use ropes for safety, I thought of the many hardships endured by the early explorers when they came into the Oregon country.

Having made a careful study of a number of their diaries, and acquainted myself with the early history of this region, I decided to write a simple story, beginning with the creation of the mountains and ending with the completion of America's Great Highway through the Cascade Mountains to the Sea.

There were three ways of entering the Oregon country from the East in pioneer days. I studied carefully to find out who had written the most interesting accounts, and have quoted from three of them verbatim. Their experiences were similar to many others whose hardships were no doubt as great. I chose Mrs. Whitman's story of the trip down the Columbia by Indian canoe to Fort Vancouver, and Mrs. Elizabeth Dickson Smith Geer's pathetic account of the experience of one among many who used the log rafts, the portage, and the Hudson's Bay batteau. Joel Palmer was chosen to tell of the trip made across the Cascade Range south of Mount Hood before the road was built. Information of great value was obtained from the Oregon Historical Society, and I am indebted to George H. Himes for his many courtesies. Frederick V. Holman, H. H. Riddell, J. C. Ainsworth, Marshall Dana, L. A. McArthur, Robert R. Rankin and Frank J. Smith also contributed to the historical value of this work.

I wish to thank George F. Holman for the work of illuminating the dedication. To Mrs. Josiah Myrick, the granddaughter of Dr. John McLoughlin, I am grateful for interest and assistance.

I have quoted freely from an article written by Miss Irene Lincoln Poppleton, "Oregon's First Monopoly," which furnished much valuable data. I have frequently used the language of Theodore Winthrup, taken from the last edition of "The Canoe and the Saddle," edited by John H. Williams. I acknowledge assistance from General Hiram M. Chittenden, Mrs. Eva Emery Dye and Fred H. Sayler; also from my beloved Pastor, Dr. W. B. Hinson, whose Christian teaching has helped me greatly in my work. The influence of Professor W. M. Wilder and his sweet home has left its imprint on this book. There I have always found harmony, and his wild flower garden overlooking the city, has been a haven in time of stress.

I acknowledge the valuable literary assistance of Mrs. Ella J. Clinton and thank all who gave the use of photographs. To Fred A. Routledge, who designed the cover of this book, and to A. Burr for original sketches, I express my grateful appreciation.

To every man who had a part in the construction of the Columbia River Highway through the Cascade Mountains to the sea; from the humblest laborer, to the Governor of the great State of Oregon, I say with all my heart, "I thank you for the help you gave; we could not have succeeded without you."

Samuel Christopher Lancaster.

CONTENTS

ILLUSTRATIONS

All photographs copyrighted by those to whom they are accredited.

Twenty-five of these pictures are by the new Paget process of Color Photography. The value of every tint and shade is recorded by this means, on glass plates in negative form. The positives (also on glass) refract the light and give true colors, without the use of paint.

The scenes in this book are exact reproductions from these color pictures made by the four-color process. Infinite pains was required to accomplish this result, and it is believed that this is the closest approach to nature that man has been able to make.

THE FALLS OF MULTNOMAH—COLUMBIA RIVER HIGHWAY.

The source of this crystal stream is Larch Mountain, 4000 feet above the Highway. A foot and pony trail crosses the concrete bridge above the lower falls and follows this beautiful stream, almost to the summit of the mountain.

MT. HOOD FROM THE TOP OF LARCH MOUNTAIN
11,225 Feet in Elevation

Larch Mountain is reached by a foot and pony trail, starting from either Multnomah or Wahkeena Falls. One branch of the Trail starts from the Highway at Multnomah Falls, and after crossing the bridge spanning the Lower Falls, winds back and forth, climbing on the side of the mountain until it passes over the rim rock and enters a box canyon above Multnomah Falls. Passing out of this canyon it unites with the trail coming up from Wahkeena Falls and continues through a magnificent forest to the top of Larch Mountain, four thousand feet above, where five great mountain peaks can be seen at once, always white with snow.

Formation of the Cascade and Sierra Nevada Ranges

T HERE was a time when the waves of a nameless ocean kissed the Western slopes of the Rocky Mountains—when unborn continents lay still in the dark, cold womb of fathomless seas. Even then, far—far off shore, the voice of God was heard, and out of the boundless deep He lifted up a mighty mountain range. From North to South it rose like some leviathan stretched at full length, with head and tail touching the mainland, and the Cascade and Sierra Nevada Ranges were created, thus forming an inland sea, a thousand miles or more in length.

How fearful were the sounds! How dark the skies! The earth groaned and trembled as if in travail when this new land was born; the very foundations were broken up, and flames burst forth. The rocks were melted with fervent heat, and white hot magma streams ran down the mountain side into the sea. Steam rose in clouds—lightnings flashed—rain poured in torrents— thunders roared. The whole mass heaved, and rose, and fell, as a bosom moved with passion, until that day's work was done.

When the sun broke through the veil, it shone on a naked land, its only clothing ashes—hot ashes—blowing, drifting everywhere.

For centuries the most active volcanoes were at work. They built up mighty domes reaching into the skies, one mile, two miles, almost three miles high, until the icy- cold of the atmosphere, where they now reared their heads, exceeded the cold of ocean depths whence the uplift came.

Time first closed the smaller vents and fissures, then hushed the greater ones. When the fires from within were extinguished, perpetual snow crowned the loftier peaks.

These great snow fields moved slowly, sliding, pushing downward, producing many an avalanche, and glaciers which extended far into the lower valleys.

In their imperceptible movements these mighty glaciers wore through the lava beds in many places, cutting gashes hundreds of feet in depth, grinding to powder the older limestone and other rocks beneath them. These fragments were mingled by the hand of God with ash and other particles of the igneous mass, which He took from the very bowels of the earth. The little rivulets joined with mountain torrents to bring the product of the glaciers down into the valleys, where He spread it out, producing a soil rich in everything that ministers to man.

Then the Prince of All Gardens planted the seeds of a thousand springtimes. Some flowers He made to grow high up in the clefts of the rocks, in fields of snow. The anemone and heather He planted a little lower down, just where the trees begin; and when He came to where the earth slopes gently out in upland meadows, jeweled with sparkling waterbrooks, He gave more freely of His abundance and carpeted the earth with flowers of every tint and hue. Alpine firs He planted here and there, grouping them, and adding others as He came down into the valleys, where He made the flowering shrubs and ferns to grow in the midst of dark, cool forests of great and stately trees, the shelter of His creatures.

There is a beauty in the bare angles of the rocks which look down from the heights, where His fingers broke them. Here He rent and tore them asunder, to make room for one of earth's great rivers.

The Columbia River Highway encircles the top of the rock which is seen on the right.

SUNSET ON MOUNT ST. HELENS—FROM "SILVER STAR" IN THE CASCADE RANGE
NORTH OF THE COLUMBIA.

The most active volcanoes built up mighty domes, reaching into the skies, one mile, two miles, almost three miles high, until the icy-cold of the atmosphere, where they now reared their heads, exceeded the cold of ocean depths whence the uplift came.

LATOURELL FALLS—COLUMBIA RIVER HIGHWAY.

The sparkling waters of this clear stream fall 224 feet into a pool at the base of an overhanging cliff. The beautiful concrete bridge (page 59) was located so as to obtain the best view of this waterfall.

Formation of the Columbia River and the Gorge

ANY men have sought to know the Truth, of how this Mountain Range was parted like a curtain, permitting the mighty Columbia River to pass through, almost at the level of the sea. The story of the uplift and the Inland Sea is writ so plain that all may read. Primitive man understood; his legends tell the story. The Inland Sea found one great outlet through the Gorge of the Columbia.

With some there is a question as to whether the Gorge is the result of a gradual uplift and slow erosion, or of the sudden breaking away, of a great rock wall that was first cracked, or faulted, by a movement of the mountain range, due to some fearful convulsion of nature; after which a wall of water from this Inland Sea, almost a mile in height, tore away the sides, and widened the chasm into its present magnificent proportions.

The mind can only wonder at this mighty work of God, done in His own way, on a scale so great that man's best efforts appear but as the work of pigmies—the Panama Canal, a toy for children.

Standing at the margin of the river and looking up along the sky line, one sees the rim rock of the mountain, in many places, thousands of feet above. The crystal waterfalls, the great trees, the fresh green moss—the rocks themselves, speak of eternal youth, and it seems but yesterday that the hand of God fashioned it all.

The talus at the base of the cliffs tells a different story. We read in these masses of broken stone, that centuries on centuries have passed since they began to form, for every particle contained in them, when loosened by frost, heat or cold, fell from dizzy heights piece by piece. Striking the base of the cliffs, they sound like the ticking of the master clock, with centuries for hours. The rich growth of vegetation, almost tropical, always hastening to hide nature's secrets, soon covers them, and out of this mouldering mass provides food and shelter for both man and beast.

Early Life in the Columbia Basin

W E KNOW that the first garden that God planted eastward in Eden and the River which went out of it were beautiful beyond compare. We also know that the one planted here, and the River called by men Columbia, which goes out of it, were formed by the same hand. How long it was before He brought the living creatures after their kind and placed them in this new-made garden, we know not. Nor can we tell how long a time elapsed before He brought the several roving tribes of men into this earthly Paradise in quest of food.

A few miles west of Celilo Falls the trees begin. The landscape changes rapidly as one goes toward the sea, descending the river or ascending the Cascade Range.

Ever higher these mountains lift their heads, until five great peaks are seen at once above the timber line, "their craters healed with snow" which never leaves them.*

The Indian legends and our early history tell of plenty. Great herds of antelope and buffalo without number roamed the plains on the head waters of this kingly river. They browsed on the rich bunch grass which grew knee high over the thousands of square miles in that treeless region, which is the basin left by the ancient Inland Sea, to the east of the Cascade Range.

The Indian tribes, who loved the chase and lived for the greater part of the year on plain and mountain top were athletes, while the tribes on the western

---

*The older Indians tell us their fathers saw these mountains smoking, and some declare that fire and rocks were thrown into the very heaven. They knew St. Helens as "Lowela-clow," meaning "Big Smoke Daytime—Big Fire Night." Fremont and others also saw St. Helens smoking and report that ashes from this mountain fell in the streets of The Dalles to the depth of half an inch in 1842. Dr. Parrish saw it active on the 22d day of November, 1842. Kane saw it smoking and made a sketch of it March 26, 1847. Winthrop noticed the black spot in the snow on the southwest side of St. Helens (this being the location of the last crater). He said in 1853, "sometimes she showers her realms with a boon of hot ashes to notify them that her peace is repose not stupor; and sometimes lifts a beacon of tremulous flame by night from her summit."

On one occasion (date unknown, supposedly 1842) ashes from St. Helens fell at Fort Vancouver for three days and it was so dark at mid-day that tallow dips were burned.

HOO-SIS-MOX-MOX.

A Chief of the Palouse tribe who lived in Southeastern Washington on the Palouse River just above its junction with the Snake. He was born in 1812 and attended both the Whitman and the Spalding Mission Schools. He was a warrior of considerable fighting ability, until he came to The Dalles and informed the white people that "he would fight no more." He was drowned in the Umatilla River in 1909, aged 97.

FALLS OF SHEPPERD'S DELL—COLUMBIA RIVER HIGHWAY.

George Shepperd gave eleven acres here for a public park, because he loved it. He used to come with his wife and children to enjoy this spot and be refreshed when they were denied the privileges of church and Sunday school, because they had no road.

coast and lower Columbia River, who lived in their canoes and fed on fish, though short and stout, were experts in the water.

Fish abounded in all the streams. One family of those unnumbered throngs, that "trace their liquid paths along" this broad river, puts out to sea when still mere minnows—going on a four years' cruise. No chart or compass have they, yet when fully grown (some weighing fifty pounds or more) they come again in schools, enter the stream of their nativity, and there complete the cycle of life.

In former years the fish literally filled the rivers, and just below Celilo Falls they were so plentiful that bands of Indians from many tribes, made long journeys from the East to get this wholesome sea food, of which there was enough for all.

By that same law which governs wild beasts at the water-hole in the jungle, each came and took enough to satisfy his needs and went away. All difference, fear, hatred, or remembrance of former strife, was forgotten, while receiving this bountiful gift from God.

Today remnants of these Indian bands continue to come from different sections of the country, just as their fathers did. They stand on the jagged rocks in the rapids and spear the salmon coming up, or dip them out with nets. Many of the fish leap high out of the water below the falls in attempting the ascent of this great river.

Measureless milleniums, mystic centuries passed while God prepared this region for the coming of civilized man. Then Captain Gray, in his little bark, "Columbia-Rediviva," crossed the bar from the Pacific Ocean, and discovered the broad river, which he entered and named. A little more than one century has elapsed since those intrepid explorers, Lewis and Clark—wise men of the East—climbed over the mountains and spied out this land.

Marcus Whitman blazed the way across the continent for the first wagon wheels to cross the Rocky Mountains and to come into the Oregon country, less than a century ago. How swift has been the change since a member of Congress said to Marcus Whitman, "There cannot be made a wagon road over the Mountains; Sir George Simpson says so," whereat the intrepid pioneer replied, "There is a wagon road, for I have made it."

Only seventy-three years have elapsed since Fremont made his first expedition. There are men and women now living in our Northwest who participated in the Indian wars of the '50's, and escaped massacre and death by narrow margins, enduring untold hardships, and overcoming obstacles apparently insurmountable.

Theodore Winthrop came from California to Portland, a city of fifteen hundred souls, in 1853. He saw the beauty of this country, loved the great mountains, and admired the Gorge of the Columbia. Writing to his sister, he said, "There is a feeling of grandeur connected wth the mountains and forests and the great continental river of this country that belongs to nothing in the land of gold. The Columbia is most imposing in its lower course, a great, broad, massive stream. Its scenery has a breadth and a wild power every way worthy of it. It will bear cultivation admirably; also and sometime—a thousand years hence—the beauty of its highly finished shores will be exquisite. * * * It is only lately in the development of man's comprehension of nature, that Mountains have been recognized as our noblest friends, our most exalting and inspiring comrades, our grandest emblems of Divine Power and Divine Peace. * * * Our race has never yet come into contact with great mountains as companions of daily life, nor felt that daily development of the finer and more comprehensive senses which these signal factors of nature compel. This is an influence of the future."*

Mr. James J. Hill, the empire builder, is continually calling to the people of the Northwest to "grow into the greatness of their natural surroundings." If the people of Oregon would do this in all respects, physically, morally, spiritually, look at the mountains, and behold! what Giants they could be!

*"The Canoe and the Saddle," edited by John H. Williams.

DR. JOHN McLOUGHLIN.
Taken from a daguerreotype of Dr. John McLoughlin, made in 1856, about a year before his death. The original daguerreotype belongs to Mrs. Josiah Myrick of Portland, Oregon, a granddaughter of Dr. McLoughlin.

The Fur Traders

THE Beaver and the Fur Traders played an important part in the early development of the Oregon country.

Following closely the exploration by Lewis and Clark, the Astor Expedition undertook an enterprise of great moment at Astoria. This was quickly ended however by competition and chicanery.

The North-West Company, which accomplished the downfall of the Astors, soon found a strong competitor in the Hudson's Bay Company—the nucleus and the conservators of British interests on the Pacific Coast.

Frequent clashes occurred between the men employed by the Canadian and the English Companies. The British Government practically commanded the warring factions to reach some satisfactory agreement, and as a result the Hudson's Bay Company absorbed the North-West Company.

Fortunately for American interests Dr. McLoughlin was placed in charge of the Hudson's Bay post, which he established at Fort Vancouver.

Dr. McLoughlin stands out as the pioneer of pioneers. He was large in body, mind, and soul. He understood the North American Indians and ruled them wisely and well. In the selection of Fort Vancouver as the base of his operations, he showed great insight, for it was the center of Indian life west of the Cascade Range, and in close touch with all Indians between the Cascade and the Rocky Mountains in the Columbia River Basin. Vancouver was at the head of navigation for ocean going vessels, which met the Montreal Express laden with furs. On the return trip the Montreal Express* took into the interior articles for barter and exchange.

Dr. McLoughlin was the first Hudson's Bay factor to undertake the cultivation of the soil and the raising of poultry, cattle and hogs. Heretofore grain and other produce had been sent out from England to supply the different trading posts.

---

*Leaving Montreal in May the Express came through the Great Lakes by steamer, then up the Canadian rivers to the headwaters of the Saskatchewan, crossing the Rocky Mountains before the snows of winter fell. This company of hardy men numbering sixty souls then descended the great Columbia River to Fort Vancouver.

Early Missionaries

The early missionaries who entered the Oregon Country in answer to the Macedonian call of the Nez Perces, were received kindly by Dr. McLoughlin. They came first to Fort Vancouver, where they rested and were

REVEREND JASON LEE

refreshed, before going to their chosen fields of labor. All of the missionaries were greatly impressed by what they saw, and many of them remained at the Fort during the winter months studying the Indians and their customs. The original letters, diaries, journals and publications of these early missionaries tell of the wonderful kindness and generosity of Dr. McLoughlin, who would accept no pay for fare or merchandise supplied them, and who on at least one occasion gave a substantial purse in aid of the work of the missionaries.

The first to come were the Reverends Jason and Daniel Lee in 1834. On preaching his first sermon at Fort Vancouver, Reverend Jason Lee made the following notation in his diary: "Sunday, 28th Sept., 1834, A. M. Assayed to preach to a mixed congregation. * * * Am thankful that I have been permitted to plead the cause of God on this side the Rocky Mountains, where the banners of Christ were never before unfurled. Great God, grant that it may not be in vain, but may some fruit appear even from the feeble attempt to labour for Thee."

On October sixteenth of the following year Reverend Samuel Parker reached Fort Vancouver and was the guest of Dr. McLoughlin. He took up his residence at Fort Vancouver for the winter, and on November 24th, 1835, he visited the falls of the Willamette. He hired eight naked Clough-e-wall-hah Indians to carry the canoe around the falls; climbing to a point of vantage he looked upon the beautiful scene and soliloquized thus—"I can

REVEREND SAMUEL PARKER

hardly persuade myself that this river had for many thousand years, poured its water continually down these falls without having facilitated the labor of man. * * * I took out my watch to see if it was not the hour for the ringing of the bells. It was two o'clock, and all was still, except the roar of the falling water. I called to recollection, that in the year 1809 I stood by the falls of Genesee river, and all was silence except the roar of the cataract. But it is not so now; for Rochester stands where I then stood."

The vision of Reverend Samuel Parker is now a reality. In the short span of eighty years we see the beautiful Willamette Valley in a high state of cultivation, towns and cities dot it here and there, while the harnessed waters drive the wheels of commerce and send the lightnings on their way to do man's bidding. Mr. Parker took his final departure on the steamship Beaver on June 18th, 1836, as she "was commencng her first voyage upon the Pacific, under the power of steam."

The Beaver was the second steam vessel to cross the Atlantic ocean
and the first to enter the Pacific.

The next to come were Dr. Marcus Whitman and his bride, accompanied by Reverend H. H. Spalding and his young wife; they arrived at the Fort on September 12th of the same year. Mrs. Whitman and Mrs. Spalding remained at the Fort while their husbands returned to select the site of the new Whitman Mission, near Walla Walla, and to erect the necessary buildings.

Life at Fort Vancouver

Many notable personages visited Fort Vancouver in those early days—among them scientists and artists. Messrs. Nuttall, Townsend, Kane and others have told us of its culture and refinement. Through them we learn something of the masterful way in which Dr. McLoughlin dealt with the many different tribes of Indians—part of a wild race of human beings, who realized that they were being robbed of their best hunting and fishing grounds by the incoming tide of civilization.

While at Fort Vancouver Mrs. Whitman completed her journal of the trip across the Continent and sent it to Dr. Whitman's relatives in the State of New York, stating that he "had been pressed above measure with care, labors, and anxieties all the way."

She relates her interesting story in a style most charming, and we can do no better than to quote from her diary as she tells of the trip taken down the Columbia River in the olden days from Fort Walla Walla to Fort Vancouver. Under date of September seventh, 1836, she says: "We set sail from Walla Walla yesterday at 2 P. M. Our boat is an open one, manned with six oarsmen and a steersman."

"I enjoy it much; it is a very pleasant change in our manner of traveling. The Columbia is a beautiful river.

Its waters are clear as crystal, and smooth as a sea of glass, exceeding in beauty the Ohio; but the scenery on each side of it is very different. There is no timber to be seen, but there are high perpendicular banks of rocks in some places, while rugged bluffs and plains of sand in others, are all that greets the eye. We sailed until near sunset, when we landed, pitched our tents, supped our tea, bread and butter, boiled ham and potatoes, committed ourselves to the care of a kind Providence, and retired to rest.

"8th.—Came last night quite to the Chute (above The Dalles*), a fall in the river not navigable. There we slept, and this morning made the portage. All were obliged to land, unload, carry our baggage, and even the boat, for half a mile. I had frequently seen the picture of the Indians carrying a canoe, but now I saw the reality. We found plenty of Indians here to assist in making the portage. After loading several with our baggage and sending them on, the boat was capsized and placed upon the heads of about twenty of them, who marched off with it with perfect ease. Below the main fall of the water are rocks, deep, narrow channels, and many frightful precipices. We walked deliberately among the rocks, viewing the scene with astonishment, for this once beautiful river seemed to be cut up and destroyed by these huge masses of rock. Indeed, it is difficult to find where the main body of the water passes. In high water we are told that these rocks are all covered with water, the river rising to such an astonishing height.

"After paying the Indians for their assistance, which was a twist of tobacco about the length of a finger to each, we reloaded, went on board, sailed about two miles, and stopped for breakfast. This was done to get away from a throng of Indians. Many followed us, however, to assist in making another portage, three miles below this.

"Sept. 9th.—We came to The Dalles just before noon. Here our boat was stopped by two rocks of immense size and height, all the water of the river passes between them in a very narrow channel, and with great rapidity. Here we were obliged to land and make a portage of two and a half miles, carrying the boat also. The Dalles is the

*Celilo Falls.

great resort of Indians of many tribes for taking fish. We did not see many, however, for they had just left. * * * I was relieved from walking by the offer of a horse from a young chief. This was a kindness, for the way was mostly through the sand, and the walk would have been fatiguing."

Continuing her story of the journey in the boat Mrs. Whitman says, "We made fine progress this morning until nine o'clock, when we were met with a head wind and obliged to make shore. We met the crew last night with the Western express. This express goes from and returns to Vancouver twice a year.

"10th.—High winds and not able to move at all today.

"11th.—We came to the Cascades for breakfast—another important falls in the river, where we are obliged to make a portage of a mile. The boat was towed along by the rocks with a rope over the falls. This is another great place for salmon fishing. A boat load was just ready for Vancouver when we arrived. I saw an infant here whose head was in the pressing machine. This was a pitiful sight. Its mother took great satisfaction in unbinding and showing its naked head to us. The child lay upon a board between which and its head was a squirrel skin. On its forehead lay a small square cushion, over which was a bandage drawn tight around, pressing its head against the board. In this position it is kept three or four months or longer, until the head becomes a fashionable shape. There is a variety of shapes among them, some being sharper than others. I saw a child about a year old whose head had been recently released from pressure, as I supposed from its looks. All the back part of it was a purple color, as if it had been sadly bruised. We are told that this custom is wearing away very fast. There are only a few tribes of this river who practice it.†

"Sept. 12th.—Breakfasted in the saw-mill, five miles from Vancouver. * * * You may be surprised to hear of a saw-mill here, when I said there was no timber on the Columbia. Since we passed the Cascade the scene is changed, and we are told there is timber all the way to the Coast.

---

†See Appendix C, Flatheads.

"Eve.—We are now at Vancouver, the New York of the Pacific Ocean. Our first sight, as we approached the fort, was two ships in the harbor, one of which, the Neriade, Captain Royal, had just arrived from London. The Columbia, Captain Dandy, came last May, and has since been to the Sandwich Islands, and returned. * * * What a delightful place this is; what a contrast to the rough, barren sand plains, through which we had so recently passed. Here we find fruit of every description, apples, peaches, grapes, pears, plums, and fig trees in abundance; also cucumbers, melons, beans, peas, beets, cabbage, tomatoes and every kind of vegetables too numerous to mention. Every part is very neat and tastefully arranged, with fine walks, lined on each side with strawberry vines. At the opposite end of the garden is a good summer house covered with grape vines. Here I must mention the origin of these grapes and apples. A gentleman, twelve years ago, while at a party in London, put the seeds of the grapes and apples which he ate into his vest pocket. Soon afterwards he took a voyage to this country and left them here. And now they are greatly multiplied.†

"After promenading as much as we wished, and returning, we were met by Mrs. Copendel, a lady from England, who arrived in the ship Columbia, last May, and Miss Maria, daughter of Dr. McLoughlin, quite an interesting young lady. After dinner we were introduced to Rev. Dr. Beaver and lady, a clergyman of the Church of England, who arrived last week in the ship Neriade. This is more than we expected when we left home—that we should be privileged with the acquaintance and society of two English ladies. Indeed, we seem to be nearly allied to old England, for most of the gentlemen of the company are from there or Scotland.

"13th.—This morning, visited the school to hear the children sing. It consists of about fifty-one children, who have French fathers and Indian mothers. All the laborers here are Canadian-French with Indian wives. * * * French is the prevailing language here. English is spoken only by a few.

---

†One of the apple trees is still growing at Vancouver and bearing fruit.

BRIDAL VEIL FALLS—COLUMBIA RIVER HIGHWAY.

This beautiful mountain stream is the only one along this great thoroughfare that has been harnessed. It is used to convey lumber down the mountain side in flumes. The water saws and stacks the finished product with but little help from man.

"14th.—We were invited to a ride to see the farm. Have ridden fifteen miles this afternoon. We visited the barns, stock, etc. They estimated their wheat crop at four thousand bushels this year. Peas the same. Oats and barley between fifteen hundred and seventeen hundred bushels each. The potato and turnip fields are large and fine. Their cattle are numerous, estimated at one thousand head in all the settlements. They have swine in abundance, also sheep and goats, but the sheep are of an inferior kind. We find also hens, turkeys and pigeons, but no geese.

"Sept. 16.—Every day we have something new to see. We went to the stores and found them filled above and below with the cargo of the two ships, all in unbroken bales. They are chiefly Indian goods, and will be sent away this fall to the several different posts of the company in the ship Neriade. We have found here every article for comfort and durability that we need, but many articles for convenience and all fancy articles are not here.

"Visited the dairy, also, where we found butter and cheese in abundance. * * * They milked between fifty and sixty cows.

"On visiting the mill we did not find it in a high state of improvement. It goes by horse power and has a wire bolt. This seemed a hard way of getting bread, but better so than no bread, or to grind by hand. The company has one at Colville that goes by water, five days' ride from Walla Walla, from whence we expect to obtain our flour, potatoes and pork. They have 300 hogs.

"Dr. McLoughlin promises to loan us enough to make a beginning and all the return he asks is that we supply other settlers in the same way. He appears desirous to offer us every facility for living in his power. No person could have received a more hearty welcome, or be treated with greater kindness than we have been since our arrival.

"* * * Sept. 22nd.—Dr. McLoughlin has put his daughter in my care, and wishes me to hear her recitations. Thus I shall have enough to do for diversion while I stay. * * *

"I have not given you a description of our eatables here. There is such a variety I know not where to begin. For breakfast we have coffee or cocoa, salt salmon and roast ducks with potatoes. When we have eaten our

COOPEY FALLS, COLUMBIA RIVER HIGHWAY.

Charles H. Coopey contributed to the success of this great enterprise by donating lands for right-of-way in order to make accessible both mountains, water falls and woodland, for rest and recreation.

supply of them, our plates are changed and we make a finish on bread and butter. For dinner we have a great variety. First we are always treated to a dish of soup, which is very good. All kinds of vegetables in use are taken, chopped fine, and put in water with a little rice, and boiled to a soup. Tomatoes are a prominent article and usually some fowl meat, duck or other kind, is cut and added. If it has been roasted once it is just as good (so the cook says), and then spiced to taste. After our soup dishes are removed, then comes a variety of meats to prove our taste. After selecting and changing, we change plates and try another if we choose, and so at every new dish have a clean plate. Roast duck is an every day dish, boiled pork, tripe, and sometimes trotters, fresh salmon or sturgeon—yea, all articles too numerous to mention. When these are set aside, a nice pudding or an apple pie is introduced. After this a water or musk melon make their appearance, and last of all cheese, bread or biscuit and butter are produced to complete the whole. But there is one article on the table which I have not yet mentioned and of which I never partake, that is wine. The gentlemen frequently drink toasts to each other, but never give us an opportunity of refusing, for they know that we belong to the Teetotal Society. We have talks about drinking wine, but no one joins our society. They have a Temperance Society here and at Wallamet, formed by Mr. Lee.

"Sept. 30th.—We are invited to ride as often as once a week for exercise, and we generally ride all the afternoon. * * *

"I sing about an hour every evening with the children, teaching them new tunes, at the request of Dr. McLoughlin. Thus I am wholly occupied, and can scarcely find as much time as I want to write. The Montreal express came this afternoon, and a general time of rejoicing it is to every one. News from distant friends, both sad and pleasing.

"Mr. Spalding has come with it, and brought a letter from my husband filled with pleasing information. The Lord has been with them since they left us and has prospered them beyond all expectations. They have each selected a location, my husband remains there to build, while Mr. Spalding comes after us. Cheering thought this, to be able to make a beginning in our pleasing work so soon."

This sweet womanly woman, filled with hope and a devotion to the cause of Christ, was soon to suffer death at the hands of those she came to save.*

The fertile fields of waving grain, the beautiful garden, filled with vegetables, fruits, and flowers of every kind, attracted all who came to Fort Vancouver, for here was an actual demonstration of the fertility of the soil, and its adaptability to the needs of civilized man.

"Dr. McLoughlin had encouraged Jason and Daniel Lee to go South into the Willamette Valley and establish their mission, and they had begun to teach the Indians and show them how to cultivate the soil."

The flower gardens at old Fort Vancouver served an added purpose in the spring of 1837, for Jason Lee met his sweetheart Anna Pittman there. They strolled about "the fine walks, lined with strawberry vines" and sat for many an hour in the "good summer house covered with grape vines at the opposite end of the garden." When their hearts were linked for life, they took their way up the beautiful Willamette River, now full to the brim. The high beaked Indian canoe skimmed the surface of the clear blue waters and bore them on beyond the roaring "falls of the Multnomah"† which sang a song of welcome as they passed up the stream to the Lee Mission, established in the fall of 1834, ten miles North of the present city of Salem. Here they were married by the Reverend Daniel Lee, July 16th, 1837, and the loneliness of labor without that help which only a good wife gives, was ended.

No doubt these young people tried to make a garden of their own, equal if not superior to the one they reveled in at Fort Vancouver. The Whitmans and the Spaldings with their young wives did likewise in their chosen fields, and it is plain to see that the good seeds sown by Dr. McLoughlin bore fruit, yes! an hundred fold. The missionaries told a waiting world about it, and this, coupled with the agitation in Congress over the "Oregon Question," turned the great tide of immigration to the Oregon country and the Willamette Valley.

---

*See Whitman Massacre. Appendix B.
†See Appendix D. Indians and River called Multnomah.

MIST FALLS, COLUMBIA RIVER HIGHWAY.

The water falling from a great height is broken into spray and mist. It is blown here and there by the wind. Sometimes it is carried away at a right angle to the cliff, and again it is blown straight up in the air, disappearing in vapor.

"I carry my babe and lead, or rather carry another through the snow, mud and water almost to my knees."

The Struggle to Possess the Land

The plain statement of actual facts which the early explorers of the Oregon country related, concerning the forests of great trees, the fertile soil and the snow-capped mountains, the many waterfalls and broad rivers, charmed like magic, and drew as a loadstone—for truth is better than fiction.

The New England schoolmaster has never failed to have a prominent place in the affairs of our nation. One of this profession, Hall J. Kelley, born in Maine, began to agitate the question of colonizing Oregon in 1829. He wrote a number of pamphlets and spent a considerable sum of money in promotion, as "General Agent of the American Society for Encouraging the Settlement of the Oregon Territory." Although he did not visit Oregon until 1834, in 1829 he published a rude map, which showed a portion of the peninsula between the Willamette and Columbia Rivers, laid out in forty-acre tracts.

The "Journal of an Exploring Trip Beyond the Rocky Mountains," by Rev. Samuel Parker, A. M., reached its third edition in 1842. The preaching and the many lectures of the Reverends Samuel Parker, Jason Lee, Marcus Whitman and other strong men of that time, bore fruit, and attracted the highest type of pioneer citizenship.

The first real immigration into the Oregon Country began, when a party left Peoria, Illinois, May 21st, 1839, and arrived in the Willamette Valley late in the fall. Their hardships were many, but their fortitude and faith in the future was sublime—characteristic of the large majority of those who came after, and helped to "carve an empire out of a wilderness."

Previous to the opening, in 1846, of what has since been known as the "Barlow Road," which crossed the Cascade Range south of Mt. Hood, all of the transcontinental immigration into Western Oregon came through the Columbia River Gorge. The hazards were great, and stout hearts were needed for the undertaking. Many a weary traveler, dreaming of the land of promise that lay just beyond the snow-capped Cascade Range, felt his cheeks blanch and his heart sink as he faced death many times over, and saw some of his comrades of that long journey, who had fought their way across the Rocky Mountains, go down in defeat, because they were unequal to the last great effort.

Mrs. Elizabeth Dickson Smith Geer, one of the early pioneers, best tells this story in her diary, in which she wrote each day, after all her children were asleep, and before she suffered her tired body to relax into the repose of the night:

"Dear Friends: By your request I have endeavored to keep a record of our journey from 'the States' to Oregon, though it is poorly done, owing to my having a young babe and besides a large family to do for; and, worst of all, my education is very limited:

"April 21, 1847—Commenced our journey from La Porte, Indiana, to Oregon; made 14 miles.

* * * * * * *

"October 27—Passed what is called The Dalles Mission, where two white families live among the Indians. It looks like starvation. Made ten miles. Camped on the Columbia River, where we expect to take water.

"October 28—Here are a great many immigrants in camp; some making rafts, others going down in boats, which have been sent up by speculators.

"October 29—Rained most all day. * * * Cold weather.

"October 30—Rainy day. Men making rafts. Women cooking and washing. Children crying. Indians bartering potatoes for shirts. They must have a good shirt for a half a peck of potatoes.

"October 31—Cold and rainy. Snow close by on the mountains. We should have went over the mountains with our wagons, but they are covered with snow, con-

WAHKEENA FALLS, COLUMBIA RIVER HIGHWAY.

Wahkeena means "most beautiful" in the Indian tongue. Of all the water falls seen from the great Highway none is more beautiful. Mr. S. Benson purchased more than three hundred acres, embracing Wahkeena Falls and gave it to the public for a recreation park.

Type of log raft used by pioneers between The Dalles and Cascade Locks

sequently we must go down by water and drive our cattle over the mountains.

"November 1—We are lying by, waiting for the wind to blow down stream in order that we may embark on our rafts.

"November 2—We took off our wagon wheels, laid them on the raft, placed the wagon beds on them and started. There are three families of us, Adam Polk, Russell Welch and ourselves, on 12 logs, 18 inches through, and 40 feet long. The water runs 3 inches over our raft.

"November 3—We are floating down the Columbia. Cold and disagreeable weather.

"November 4—Rain all day. Laid by for the water to become calm. We clambered up a side hill among the rocks and built a fire and tried to cook and warm ourselves and children, while the wind blew and the waves rolled beneath.

"November 5—Still lying by waiting for calm weather. Mr. Polk is very sick.

"November 6—Laid by until noon waiting for the waves to quit rolling, but finally put out in rough water. Made 6 miles and landed safe.

THE FALLS OF ONEONTA, COLUMBIA RIVER HIGHWAY.

Hidden in the depths of Oneonta Gorge this charming water fall makes its last great leap from the mountain side above. The clear cold water falling into the narrow gorge produces strong air currents and makes this a delightful place for a day's outing in the summer time.

"November 7—Put out in rough water. Moved a few miles. The water became so rough that we were forced to land. No one to man the raft but my husband and the oldest son of 16 years. Russell Welch and our youngest boys were driving our cattle over the mountains. Here we lay smoking our eyes, burning our clothes, and trying to keep warm. We have plenty of wood, but the wind takes away the warmth.

"November 8—Finds us still lying at anchor waiting for the wind to fall. We have but one day's provision ahead of us here. We can see snow on the top of the mountains, whose rocky heights reach to the clouds by times. A few Indians call on us and steal something from us, but we are not afraid of them. Cold weather— my hands are so numb that I can scarcely write.

"November 9—Finds us still in trouble. Waves dashing over our raft and we already stinting ourselves with provisions. My husband started this morning to hunt provisions. Left no man with us, except our oldest boy. It is very cold. The icicles are hanging from our wagon beds to the water. Tonight about dusk Adam Polk expired. No one with him but his wife and myself. We sat up all night with him while the waves was dashing below.

"November 10—Finds us still waiting for calm weather. My husband returned at two o'clock. Brought 50 pounds of beef on his back 12 miles, which he had bought from another company. By this time the water became calm and we started once more, but the wind soon began to blow and we were forced to land. My husband and boy were an hour and a half after dark getting the raft landed and made fast while the water ran knee deep over our raft, the wind blew, and was freezing cold. We women and children did not attempt to get out of our wagons tonight.

"November 11—Laid by most all day. Started this evening, ran about 3 miles and landed after dark. Here we found Welch and our boys with our cattle, for they could be driven no further on this side for mountains. Here was a ferry for the purpose of ferrying immigrants' cattle.

"November 12—Ferried our cattle over the river and buried Mr. Polk. Rain all day. We are living entirely on beef.

HORSETAIL FALLS, COLUMBIA RIVER HIGHWAY.

Coming from a great height the water shoots downward with a high velocity as it passes over the face of the moss covered cliff. It resembles the tail of a horse. There is excellent fishing in the pool at the base of the falls.

[43]

"November 13—We got the ferry men to shift our load in their boat and take us down to the falls, where we found quite a town of people waiting for their cattle to pull them around the falls. Rain all day.

"November 14—Unloaded the boat, put our wagons together. Drizzly weather.

"November 15—Rainy day.

"November 16—Rain all day.

"November 17—Rainy weather.

"November 18—My husband is sick. It rains and snows. We start this morning around the falls with our wagon. We have 5 miles to go. I carry my babe and lead, or rather carry another through the snow, mud and water almost to my knees. It is the worst road that a team could possibly travel. I went ahead with my children and I was afraid to look behind me for fear of seeing the wagons turn over into the mud and water with everything in them. My children gave out with cold and fatigue, and could not travel, and the boys had to unhitch the oxen and bring them and carry the children on to camp. I was so cold and numb that I could not tell by the feeling that I had any feet at all. We started this morning at sunrise and did not get to camp until after dark, and there was not one dry thread on one of us—not even my babe. I had carried my babe and I was so fatigued that I could scarcely speak or step. When I got here I found my husband lying in Welch's wagon, very sick. He had brought Mrs. Polk down the day before and was taken sick here. We had to stay up all night tonight for our wagons are left half way back. I have not told half we suffered. I am not adequate to the task. Here was some hundreds camped, waiting for boats to come and take them down the Columbia to Vancouver or Portland or Oregon City.

"November 19—My husband is sick and can have but little care. Rain all day.

"November 20—Rain all day. It is almost an impossibility to cook and quite so to keep warm or dry. I froze or chilled my feet so that I cannot wear a shoe, so I have to go around in the cold weather barefooted.

"November 21—Rain all day. The whole care of everything falls upon my shoulders. I cannot write any more at present.

THE FALLS OF McCORD CREEK, COLUMBIA RIVER HIGHWAY.

Situated near the heart of the Cascade Range this mountain torrent has a picturesque setting. It is wild and beautiful; typical of the "Columbia Gorge Park" which has been set aside by the National Government for public recreation.

Hudson's Bay Batteau, used on the Columbia River, below Cascades

"November 27—Embarked once more on the Columbia on a flat boat. Rain all day, though the waves threatened hard to sink us. Passed Fort Vancouver in the night. Landed a mile below. My husband has never left his bed since he was taken sick.

"November 28—Still moving on the water.

"November 29—Landed at Portland on the Willamette, 12 miles above the mouth, at 11 o'clock at night.

*   *   *   *

"February 1—Rain all day. This day my dear husband, my last remaining friend, died."

What a pitiful story of hardship and suffering! Yet it was only one of many such.

Those who braved the terrors of the great river and overcame the rugged mountain barriers are entitled to all honor and praise from this generation which now enjoys the fruits of their labors.

In the fall of 1845 a company of emigrants started over the Cascade Range south of Mount Hood, choosing rather to suffer the hardships of the steep and rugged ascent of the mountain, and the perilous descent on the western slope, than to risk their all on a raft of logs while

THE DIVIDE IN THE CASCADE RANGE, COLUMBIA RIVER HIGHWAY.

In passing through the Columbia River Gorge the early pioneers risked their lives, and it is fitting that a suitable monument should be erected at this point, on top of this rock, representing the old fashioned ox team and wagon, moulded in bronze.

making the passage down the Columbia River through the rock-bound gorge.

This company was led by Joel Palmer, a man of strong character and great determination. Born of Quaker parents, then residents of New York, though visiting in Canada at the time of Joel's birth, he spent his youth in Pennsylvania and there he was married. In 1836 he moved to Indiana and in 1844 was a member of the legislature.

The national discussion of the Oregon question at this time influenced him, and he tells us in his "Journal of Travels Over the Rocky Mountains." "Having concluded from the best information, I am able to obtain, that the Oregon Territory offers great inducements to immigrants, I determined to visit it with a view of satisfying myself in regard to it, and by ascertaining by personal observation whether its advantages were sufficient to warrant me in the effort to make it my future home. I started, accordingly, on the morning of the 16th of April, 1845, in company with Mr. Spencer Buckley. We expected to be joined by several young men from Rushville, Ind., but they all abandoned the enterprise, and gave us no other encouragement than their good wishes for our success and safety. * * *

JOEL PALMER

"September 17.—At eight o'clock this morning, the men who had left us at Grand Round for Dr. Whitman's station, joined us, accompanied by the doctor and his lady. They came in a two horse wagon, bringing with them a plentiful supply of flour, meal and potatoes. After our party had taken some refreshments, the march was resumed; our visitors accompanying us to our camp four miles down the river. * * *

"September 21.—This morning at daylight we started for the Columbia, distance three and a half miles. The river at this place is from a half to three-fourths of a mile in width. It is a beautiful stream; its waters are clear and course gently over a pebbly bottom. * * * * * *. There was something inspiring and animating in beholding this. A feeling of pleasure would animate our breasts akin to that feeling in the breast of the mariner, when after years of absence, the shores of his native land appear to view. We could scarcely persuade ourselves but that our journey had arrived at its termination. We were full of hope, and as it was understood that we had but one more difficult part of the road to surmount, we moved forward with redoubled energy; our horses and cattle were much jaded, but we believed that they could be got through or at least the greater part of them.

"The Indians were constantly paying us visits, furnishing us with vegetables, which, by the by, were quite welcome; but they would in return demand wearing apparel, until by traffic, we were left with but one suit. We were compelled to keep a sharp lookout over our kitchen furniture, as during these visits it was liable to diminish in quantity by forming an attachment towards these children of the forest, and following them off. Many of these savages were nearly naked. * * *

"September 29.—This day we traveled about five miles, which brought us to The Dalles, or Methodist Missions. Here was the end of our road, as no wagons had ever gone below this place. We found some 60 families in waiting for a passage down the river; and as there were but two small boats running to the Cascade Falls, our prospect for a speedy passage was not overly flattering.

"September 30.—This day we intended to make arrangements for our passage down the river, but we

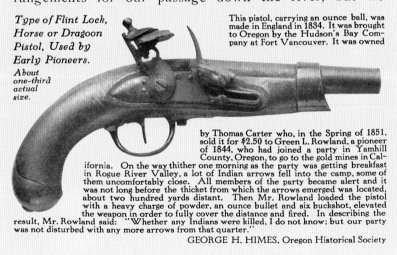

Type of Flint Lock, Horse or Dragoon Pistol, Used by Early Pioneers.
About one-third actual size.

This pistol, carrying an ounce ball, was made in England in 1834. It was brought to Oregon by the Hudson's Bay Company at Fort Vancouver. It was owned by Thomas Carter who, in the Spring of 1851, sold it for $2.50 to Green L. Rowland, a pioneer of 1844, who had joined a party in Yamhill County, Oregon, to go to the gold mines in California. On the way thither one morning as the party was getting breakfast in Rogue River Valley, a lot of Indian arrows fell into the camp, some of them uncomfortably close. All members of the party became alert and it was not long before the thicket from which the arrows emerged was located, about two hundred yards distant. Then Mr. Rowland loaded the pistol with a heavy charge of powder, an ounce bullet and six buckshot, elevated the weapon in order to fully cover the distance and fired. In describing the result, Mr. Rowland said: "Whether any Indians were killed, I do not know; but our party was not disturbed with any more arrows from that quarter."

GEORGE H. HIMES, Oregon Historical Society

found upon inquiry, that the two boats spoken of were engaged for at least ten days, and that their charges were exorbitant, and would probably absorb what little we had left to pay our way to Oregon City. We then determined to make a trip over the mountains, and made inquiries respecting its practicability of some Indians but could learn nothing definite, excepting that grass, timber and water would be found in abundance; we finally ascertained that a Mr. Barham and Mr. Nighton had, with the same object, penetrated some 20 or 35 miles into the interior, and found it impracticable. Nighton had returned, but Barham was yet in the mountains, endeavoring to force a passage; they had been absent six days, with seven wagons in their train, intending to go as far as they could, and if found to be impracticable to return and go down the river.

"We succeeded in persuading 15 families to accompany us in our trip over the mountains, and immediately made preparations for our march. On the afternoon of the 4th of October, our preparations were announced as complete, and we took up our line of march; others in the meantime had joined us, and should we fall in with Barham, our train would consist of some 30 wagons. * *

"October 3.—This morning I started on horseback in advance of the company, accompanied by one of its members. Our course led us south over a rolling, grassy plain; portions of the road were very stony. After a travel of 14 miles, we arrived at a long and steep declivity, which we descended, and after crossing the creek at its base, ascended a bluff; in the bottom are seen several small enclosures, where the Indians have cultivated the soil; a few Indian huts may be seen along this stream. Meek's company crossed the Deshute's river near the mouth of this stream, which is five miles distant. After ascending, we turned to the right, directing our course over a level, grassy plain for some five miles or more, when we crossed a running branch; five miles brought us to Stony Branch, and to scattering yellow pine timber. Here we found Barham's company of seven wagons. Barham was absent at the time, having with three others started into the mountains three days before. We remained with them all night.

THE BIRTH OF A NEW DAY.

Sunrise, and Mt. Hood from the Heights overlooking the "Rose City." No reproduction can do justice to the original view, for God alone can make it as it is; Man's best effort can only suggest an outline of its beauty.

CROWN POINT, COLUMBIA RIVER HIGHWAY.

This great rock stands 725 feet above the mile wide river. The Columbia River Highway encircles the top of it. A reinforced concrete side walk and railing extend around the outer edge of the roadway and every 20 feet there is a lamp post with its electrolier (see page 56).

"October 4.—This morning myself and companions, with a scanty supply of provisions for a few days' journey, started on a westerly course into the mountains, from the open ground we could see Mt. Hood. Our object was to go south and near to this peak. * * *

"We then ascended the mountain and as our stock of provisions were barely sufficient to last us through the day, it was found necessary to return to camp. * * * We retraced our steps to where we had struck the bluff, and followed down a short distance, where we found the mountain of sufficiently gradual descent to admit of the passage of teams; we could then follow up the bottom toward Mt. Hood, and as we supposed that this peak was a dividing ridge we had reasonable ground to believe that we could get through. We then took our trail in the direction of camp; and late in the evening, tired and hungry, we arrived at Rock Creek, where we found our company and camped. Barham had not yet returned, but we resolved to push forward.

"October 6.—We remained in camp. As the grazing was poor in the timber, and our loose cattle much trouble to us, we determined to send a party with them to the settlement. The Indians had informed us that there was a trail to the north, which ran over Mount Hood, and thence to Oregon City. This party was to proceed up one of the ridges until they struck this trail, and then follow it to the settlement. Two families decided upon going with this party, and as I expected to have no further use for my horse, I sent him with them. They were to procure provisions and assistance, and meet  us on the way. We had forwarded, by a company of cattle-drivers from The Dalles, which started for the settlement on the first of the month, a request that they would send us provisions and assistance; but as we knew nothing of their whereabouts, we had little hope of being benefited by them. * * *

"October 7.—Early in the morning, the party designated to drive our loose cattle made their arrangements, and left us. And as we supposed our stock of provisions was insufficient to supply us until these men returned, we dispatched a few men to The Dalles for a beef and some wheat; after which, we divided our company so as that a portion were to remain and take charge of the camp. A sufficient number were to pack provisions, and the remainder were to be engaged in opening the road. All being ready, each one entered upon the duty assigned him with an alacrity and willingness that showed a full determination to prosecute it to completion, if possible. On the evening of the 10th, we had opened a road to the top of the mountain, which we were to descend to the branch of the Deshutes. The side of the mountain was covered with a species of laurel bush, and so thick, that it was almost impossible to pass through it, and as it was very dry we set it on fire. We passed down and encamped on the creek, and during the night the fire had nearly cleared the road on the side of the mountain.

"On the morning of October 11th, a consultation was had, when it was determined that Mr. Barham, Mr. Lock, and myself, should go in advance, and ascertain whether we could find a passage over the main dividing ridge. In the meantime, the remainder of the party were to open the road up the creek bottom as far as they could, or until our return. We took some provisions in our pockets, an axe, and one rifle, and started. We followed up this branch about fifteen miles, when we reached a creek, coming in from the left. We followed up this for a short distance, and then struck across to the main fork; and in doing so, we came into a cedar swamp, so covered with heavy timber and brush that it was almost impossible to get through it. We were at least one hour in traveling half a mile. We struck the opening along the other fork, traveled up this about eight miles, and struck the Indian trail spoken of before, near where it comes down the mountain. The last eight miles of our course had been nearly north—a high mountain putting down between the branch and main fork. Where we struck the trail, it turned west into a wide, sandy and stony plain, of several

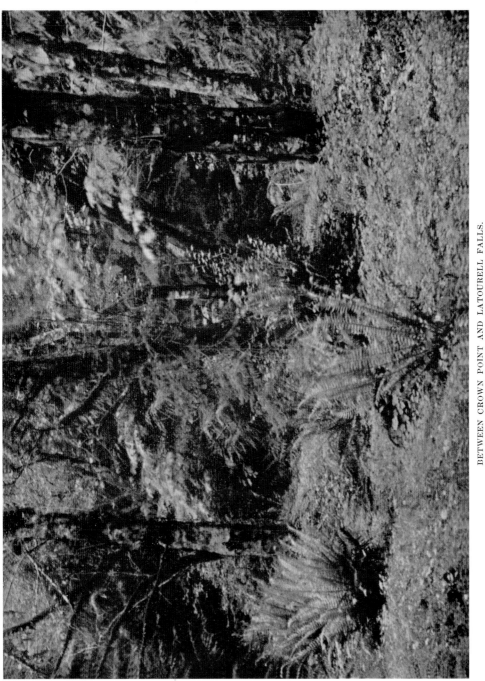

BETWEEN CROWN POINT AND LATOURELL FALLS.

The Columbia River Highway loops back and forth, paralleling itself five times, where He made the flowering shrubs and ferns to grow in the midst of dark, cool forests of great and stately trees, for the shelter of His creatures.

CROWN POINT, COLUMBIA RIVER HIGHWAY.

The Columbia River Highway as seen from Crown Point Chalet. The broad thoroughfare encircles the top of the great rock which stands 725 feet above the mile wide river. (See page 52.) The Vista House (shown on page 180) is soon to be erected in the center of the circular area.

miles in width, extending up to Mount Hood, about seven or eight miles distant, and in plain view.

"I had never before looked upon a sight so nobly grand. We had previously seen only the top of it, but now we had a view of the whole mountain. No pen can give an adequate description of this scene. The bottom which we were ascending, had a rise of about three feet to the rod. A perfect mass of rock and gravel had been washed down from the mountain. In one part of the bottom was standing a grove of dead trees, the top of which could be seen; from appearance, the surface had been filled up seventy-five or eighty feet about them. The water came tumbling down, through a little channel, in torrents. Near the upper end of the bottom, the mountains upon either side narrowed in until they left a deep chasm or gulf, where it emerged from the rocky cliffs above.

"Stretching away to the south, was a range of mountains, which from the bottom appeared to be connected with the mountain on our left. It appeared to be covered with timber far up; then a space of over two miles covered with grass; then a space of more than a mile destitute of vegetation; then commenced the snow, and continued rising until the eye was pained in looking to the top. To our right was a high range, which connected with Mount Hood, covered with timber. The timber near the snow was dead.

"We followed this trail for five or six miles, when it wound up a grassy ridge to the left—followed it up to where it connected with the main ridge; this we followed up for a mile, when the grass disappeared, and we came to a ridge entirely destitute of vegetation. It appeared to be sand and gravel, or rather, decomposed material from sandstone crumbled to pieces. Before reaching this barren ridge, we met a party of those who had started with the loose cattle, hunting for some which had strayed off. They informed us that they had lost about one-third of their cattle, and were then encamped on the west side of Mount Hood. We determined to lodge with them, and took the trail over the mountain. In the mean time, the cattle-drovers had found a few head, and traveled with us to their camp.

"Soon after ascending and winding round this barren ridge, we crossed a ravine, one or two rods in width, upon the snow, which terminated a short distance below the trail, and extended up to the top of Mount Hood. We then went around the mountain for about two miles, crossing several strips of snow, until we came to a deep canyon or gulf, cut out by the wash from the mountain above us. A precipitate cliff of rocks, at the head, prevented a passage around it. The hills were of the same material as that we had been traveling over, and were very steep.

"I judged the ravine to be three thousand feet deep. The manner of descending is to turn directly to the right, go zigzag for about one hundred yards, then turn short round, and go zigzag until you come under the place where you started from; then to the right, and so on, until you reach the base. In the bottom is a rapid stream, filled with sand. After crossing, we ascended in the same manner, went round the point of a ridge, where we struck another ravine; the sides of this were covered with grass and whortleberry bushes. In this ravine we found the camp of our friends. We reached them about dark; the wind blew a gale, and it was quite cold.

"October 12.—After taking some refreshment, we ascended the mountain, intending to head the deep ravine, in order to ascertain whether there was any gap in the mountain south of us, which would admit of a pass. From this peak, we overlooked the whole of the mountains. We followed up the grassy ridge for one mile and a half, when it became barren. My two friends began to lag behind, and show signs of fatigue; they finally stopped, and contended that we could not get round the head of the ravine, and that it was useless to attempt an ascent. But I was of a different opinion, and wished to go on. They consented, and followed for half a mile, when they sat down, and requested me to go up to the ledge, and, if we could effect a passage up and get round it, to give them a signal. I did so, and found that by climbing up a cliff of snow and ice,† for about forty feet, but not so steep but that by getting upon one cliff, and cutting holes to stand in and hold on by, it could be ascended. I gave the signal, and they came up. In the meantime, I had cut and carved

---

†This wall of ice was no doubt the nose, or lower extremity, of Zig-Zag glacier, which extends to the top of Mount Hood. Elevation, 11,225 feet.

CONCRETE BRIDGE AT LATOURELL FALLS.

There are three arches eighty feet in length; the bridge is one hundred feet in height. The Falls of Latourell can be seen from the bridge, pouring their shining waters over the vertical wall of a basalt cliff, where the rock is formed into pentagonal shapes which hang down like icicles. The Giant's Causeway of the Irish Coast is well known, but it offers no better example of rock crystallization.

COLUMBIA RIVER HIGHWAY NEAR CROWN POINT.

The smooth surface of the finished pavement is delightful to drive over. The roadway forms a suitable frame to the beautiful picture and adds a charm to the landscape. Note how the limbs of the trees are effected by the prevailing east winds.

For the latest releases and
thousands of books in print,
fill out the back of this card
and return it today!

SCHIFFER PUBLISHING LTD
4880 LOWER VALLEY ROAD
ATGLEN, PA 19310-9717 USA

WE HOPE THAT YOU ENJOY THIS BOOK...and that it will occupy a proud place in your

library. We would like to keep you informed about other publications from Schiffer Books.

Please return this card with your requests and comments. **(Please print clearly in ink.)**

Note: We don't share our mailing list with anyone.

Title of Book Purchased _____

☐ Purchased at: _____ ☐ received as a gift

Comments or ideas for books you would like to see us publish: _____

Your Name: _____

Address _____

City _____ State _____ Zip _____ Country _____

E-mail Address _____

Please provide your email address to receive announcements of new releases

☐ Please send me a **free** *Schiffer Antiques, Collectibles, & the Arts*
☐ Please send me a **free** *Schiffer Woodcarving, Woodworking, and Crafts Catalog*
☐ Please send me a **free** *Schiffer Military, Aviation, and Automotive History Catalog*
☐ Please send me a **free** *Schiffer Lifestyle, Design, and Body, Mind, & Spirit Catalog*

See our most current books on the web at **www.schifferbooks.com**

Contact us at: Phone: 610-593-1777; Fax: 610-593-2002; or E-mail: info@schifferbooks.com

SCHIFFER BOOKS ARE CURRENTLY AVAILABLE FROM YOUR BOOKSELLER

K: user\do\wp\basic\bounceback

Printed in China

my way up the cliff, and when up to the top was forced
to admit that it was something of an undertaking; but as
I had arrived safely at the top of the cliff, I doubted not
but they could accomplish the same task, and as my moccasins were worn out, and the soles of my feet exposed
to the snow, I was disposed to be traveling, and so left
them to get up the best way they could. After proceed-
ing about one mile upon the snow, continually winding
up, I began to despair of seeing my companions. I came
to where a few detached pieces of rock had fallen from
the ledge above and rolled down upon the ice and snow,
(for the whole mass is more like ice than snow); I clambered upon one of these, and waited half an hour. I
then rolled stones down the mountain for half an hour;
but as I could see nothing of my two friends, I began to
suspect that they had gone back, and crossed in the trail.
I then went round to the southeast side, continually ascending, and taking an observation of the country south,
and was fully of the opinion that we could find a passage
through.*

"The waters of this deep ravine, and of numerous
ravines to the northwest, as well as the southwest, form
the heads of Big Sandy and Quicksand Rivers, which
empty into the Columbia, about twenty-five or thirty
miles below the Cascade Falls. I could see down this
stream some twelve or fifteen miles, where the view was
obstructed by a high range coming round from the northwest side, connecting by a low gap with some of the spurs
from this peak. All these streams were running through
such deep chasms, that it was impossible to pass them
with teams. To the south, were two ranges of mountains,
connecting by a low gap with this peak, and winding
round until they terminated near Big Sandy. I observed
that a stream, heading near the base of this peak and running southeast for several miles, there appeared to turn

*"The opinion heretofore entertained, that this peak could not be ascended to
its summit, I found to be erroneous. I, however, did not arrive at the highest
peak, but went sufficiently near to prove its practicability. I judge the diameter
of this peak, at the point where the snow remains the year round, to be about three
miles. At the head of many of the ravines, are perpendicular cliffs of rocks,
apparently several thousand feet high; and in some places those cliffs rise so
precipitately to the summit, that a passage around is impracticable. I think the
southern side affords the easiest ascent. The dark strips observable from a distance,
are occasioned by blackish rock, so precipitous as not to admit of the snow lying upon
it. The upper strata are of gray sandstone, and seem to be of original formation.
There is no doubt that any of the snow peaks upon this range can be ascended to the
summit."

to the west. This I judged to be the head waters of Clackamis, which empties into the Willamette, near Oregon City; but the view was hid by a high range of mountains putting down in that direction. A low gap seemed to connect this stream, or some other, heading in this high range, with the low bottoms immediately under the base of this peak. I was of the opinion that a pass might be found between this peak and the first range of mountains, by digging down some of the gravel hills; and if not, there would be a chance of passing between the first and second ranges, through this gap to the branch of Clackamis; or, by taking some of the ranges of mountains and following them down, could reach the open ground near the Willamette, as there appeared to be spurs extending in that direction. I could also see a low gap in the direction from where we crossed the small branch, coming up the creek on the 11th, towards several small prairies south of us. It appeared, that if we could get a road opened to that place, our cattle could range about these prairies until we could find a passage for the remainder of the way.

"The day was getting far advanced, and we had no provisions, save each of us a small biscuit; and knowing that we had at least twenty-five miles to travel, before reaching those working on the road, I hastened down the mountain. I had no difficulty in finding a passage down; but I saw some deep ravines and crevices in the ice which alarmed me, as I was compelled to travel over them. The snow and ice had melted underneath, and in many places had left but a thin shell; some of them had fallen in and presented hideous looking caverns. I was soon out of danger, and upon the east side of the deep ravine I saw my two friends slowly winding their way up the mountain. They had gone to the foot of the ledge, and as they wore boots, and were much fatigued, they abandoned the trip, and returned down the mountain to the trail, where I joined them. We there rested awhile, and struck our course for one of the prairies which we had seen from the mountain. On our way we came to a beautiful spring of water, surrounded with fine timber; the ground was covered with whortleberry bushes, and many of them hanging full of fruit, we halted, ate our

SHEPPERD'S DELL LOOKING WEST.

The white arch of concrete bridges a chasm one hundred and fifty feet in width and one hundred and forty feet in depth. The roadway is cut out of solid rock above the main line tracks of the O.-W. R. & N. Company, which follows the valley of the broad Columbia. A sparkling waterfall leaps from beetling cliffs and speaks of George Shepperd's love for the beautiful, and the good that men can do.

LOOKING OUT OF SHEPPERD'S DELL, COLUMBIA RIVER HIGHWAY.

Standing on the foot path near a sparkling water fall (see page 20), the eye looks through the white arch of concrete which supports the Columbia River Highway and spans this narrow gorge. The roadway is 140 feet above the railroad track. Crown Point, four miles distant, is seen at the upper left hand corner of the picture.

biscuit, gathered berries, and then proceeded down the mountain. * * *

"After traveling about ten miles, we reached the prairie. We now took our course for camp, intending to strike through the gap to the mouth of the small branch; but we failed in finding the right shute, and came out into the bottom, three miles above where we had first struck the cattle or Indian trail. We then took down the bottom, and arrived in camp about eleven o'clock at night; and although not often tired, I was willing to acknowledge that I was near being so. I certainly was hungry, but my condition was so much better than that of my two friends, that I could not murmur. Our party had worked the road up to the small branch, where they were encamped.

"On the morning of the 13th of October we held a consultation, and determined upon the future movements of the company. The party designated to bring us provisions had performed that service; but the amount of our provisions was nearly exhausted and many of the party had no means of procuring more. Some of them began to despair of getting through this season. Those left with the camp were unable to keep the cattle together, and a number of them had been lost. The Indians had stolen several horses, and a variety of mishaps occurred, such as would necessarily follow from a company so long remaining in one position. They were now on a small creek, five miles from Stony Hill, which we called Camp creek, and near the timber. It was impossible to keep more than one-third of the men working at the road; the remainder were needed to attend the camp and pack provisions. It was determined to send a party and view out the road, through to the open country, near the mouth of Clackamis, whilst the others were to open the road as far as the big prairie; a number sufficient to bring up the teams and loose cattle, (for a number of families with their cattle had joined since ours left, and portions of our company did not send their loose cattle,) to a grassy prairie in this bottom, and near the mouth of this creek, as the time required to pack provisions to those working on the road would be saved. All being arranged, the next thing was to designate the persons to go ahead of the party, and if found practicable to return with provisions and help; or at all events to ascertain whether the route were practicable.

"It was determined that I should undertake this trip. I asked only one man to accompany me. We took our blankets, a limited supply of provisions, and one light axe, and at eight o'clock in the morning set out. I was satisfied that the creek which we were then on, headed in the low gap, seen from Mount Hood; and the party were to open the road up this branch. But as I was to precede them, I passed up this creek for about eight or ten miles, when I discovered the low gap, went through it, and at noon arrived at the wet prairie, which we had visited the day before. The route was practicable, but would require great labor to remove the timber, and cut out the underbrush.

"We halted at the creek and took some refreshment; we then struck for the low gap between the first range of mountains running west, and the base of Mount Hood, and traveled through swamps, small prairies, brush, and heavy timber for about twelve miles, when we found the labor necessary to open a wagon road in this direction, to be greater than we could possibly bestow upon it before the rainy season. We determined to try some other route, retraced our steps six or seven miles, and then bore to the right, around the base of the mountain, when we struck into an old Indian trail. This we followed for seven or eight miles, through the gap I had seen from Mount Hood. It is a rolling bottom of about four or five miles in width, and extending from the base of Mount Hood south for ten or twelve miles. The trail wound around the mountain, but as its course was about that we wished to travel, we followed it until it ran out at the top of the mountain. We then took the ridge west, and traveled until dark; but as the moon shone bright, and the timber was not very thick, we turned an angle down the mountain to the left, to procure water. We traveled about three miles, and struck upon a small running branch; this we followed, until owing to the darkness, we were compelled to encamp, much fatigued, and somewhat disheartened.

"October 14.—At daylight we were on the way. My moccasins, which the night before had received a pair of soles, in yesterday's tramp had given way, and in traveling after night my feet had been badly snagged, so that I was in poor plight for walking; but as there was no alternative, we started down the mountain, and after traveling a

SHEPPERD'S DELL, LOOKING EAST.

The heavy stone and concrete railings protect the traveling public. The one hundred foot arch is permanent and graceful. The tract of eleven acres at this point, given by George Shepperd for a public park, is unexcelled. God made this beauty spot and gave it to a man with a great heart. Men of wealth and high position have done big things for the Columbia River Highway which will live in history; but George Shepperd, the man of small means, did his part full well.

LOOKING EAST FROM SHEPPERD'S DELL, COLUMBIA RIVER HIGHWAY.

This great pillar of basalt forms the east gateway to Shepperd's Dell. It was necessary to cut under the side of this rock in order to secure the full width of roadway and permit a good sight ahead. It is one of the many attractive features in Shepperd's Dell.

few miles I felt quite well and was able to take the lead. We traveled about three miles, when we struck a large creek which had a very rapid current, over a stony bottom. I had hoped to find a bottom of sufficient width to admit of a wagon road, but after following down this stream six miles, I was satisfied that it would not do to attempt it this season.

"The weather, which had been entirely clear for months, had through the night began to cloud up; and in the morning the birds, squirrels and every thing around, seemed to indicate the approach of a storm. I began for the first time to falter, and was at a stand to know what course to pursue. I had understood that the rainy season commenced in October, and that the streams rose to an alarming height, and I was sensible that if we crossed the branch of the Deschutes, which headed in Mount Hood, and the rainy season set in, we would not get back, and to get forward would be equally impossible; so that in either event starvation would be the result. And as I had been very active in inducing others to embark in the enterprise, my conscience would not allow me go on and thus endanger so many families. But to go back, and state to them the difficulties to be encountered, and the necessity of taking some other course, seemed to be my duty. I therefore resolved to return, and recommend selecting some suitable place for a permanent camp, build a cabin, put in such effects as we could not pack out, and leave our wagons and effects in the charge of some persons until we could return the next season, unincumbered with our families and cattle, and finish the road;—or otherwise to return to The Dalles with our teams, where we could leave our baggage in charge of the missionaries, and then descend the Columbia. And when my mind was fully made up, we were not long in carrying it into execution.

"We accordingly ascended the mountain, as it was better traveling than in the bottom. The distance to the summit was about four miles, and the way was sometimes so steep as to render it necessary to pull up by the bushes. We then traveled east until we reached the eastern point of this mountain, and descended to the bottom, the base of which we had traversed the day before. We then struck for the trail, soon found it, and followed it until it led us to the southern end of the wet prairie. We then struck for the lower gap in the direction of the camp, crossed over and descended the branch to near its mouth, where we found four of our company clearing the road, the remainder having returned to Camp creek for teams. But as we had traveled about fifty miles this day, I was unable to reach the camp.

"October 15.—This morning we all started for camp, carrying with us our tools and provisions. We reached camp about two P. M. * * * Mr. Ruffner, and lady, concluded to pack out what articles they could, and leave a man to take charge of the teams and cattle, until he returned with other horses. * * * Mr. Barham and Mr. Rector made a proposition to continue working the road until the party could go to and return from the valley; they agreeing to insure the safety of the wagons, if compelled to remain through the winter, by being paid a certain per cent upon the valuation. This proposition was thought reasonable by some, and it was partially agreed to. And as there were some who had no horses with which to pack out their families, they started on foot for the valley, designing to look out a road as they passed along. Some men in the mean time were to remain with the camp. * * * This all being agreed upon, arrangements were made accordingly.

"October 16.—The morning was lowering, with every indication of rain. Messrs. Barham and Rector started on the trip. All hands were making arrangements for moving the camp. In the mean time Mr. Ruffner and his lady, and Mrs. Thompson, were ready to start. I joined them, and we again set out for the settlement. * * *

"On the morning of the 17th of October after our horses had filled themselves, we packed up and started. It was still raining. We followed up this bottom to the trail, and then pursued the trail over Mount Hood. Whilst going over this mountain the rain poured down in torrents, it was foggy, and very cold. We arrived at the deep ravine at about four P. M., and before we ascended the opposite bank it was dark; but we felt our way over the ridge and round the point to the grassy run. Here was grazing for our tired horses, and we dismounted. Upon the side of the mountain, where were a few scattered trees, we found some limbs and sticks, with which we succeeded

FALLS OF MULTNOMAH WHEN AUTUMN TINTS THE FOLIAGE.

There are higher waterfalls and falls of greater volume, but there are none more beautiful than Multnomah. The setting is ideal. It is pleasing to look upon; and in every mood, it charms like magic, it woos like an ardent lover; it refreshes the soul, and invites to loftier, purer things. The Columbia River Highway crosses the stream on a beautiful concrete arch.

FALLS OF MULTNOMAH, COLUMBIA RIVER HIGHWAY.

When God made this world He utilized the forces of nature, and produced many beautiful things for the enjoyment of His children. No imaginable "Dream Garden" could equal the splendor of this wonderful place, which is often declared to be "too beautiful to be real."

[72]

in getting a little fire. We then found a few sticks and constructed a tent, covering it with blankets, which protected our baggage and the two women. Mr. Ruffner and myself stood shivering in the rain around the fire, and when daylight appeared, it gave us an opportunity to look at each others' lank visages. Our horses were shivering with the cold, the rain had put out our fire, and it seemed as though every thing had combined to render us miserable. After driving our horses round awhile, they commenced eating; but we had very little to eat, and were not troubled much in cooking it.

"October 18.—As soon as our horses had satisfied themselves we packed up and ascended the mountain over the ridge. * * * The rain was falling in torrents, and it was so foggy that we could barely see the trail. * * *

"We soon saw a large band of cattle coming up the mountain, and in a short time met a party of men following them. They had started from The Dalles about eight days before, and encamped that night four or five miles below, and as it was a barren spot, their cattle had strayed to the mountain to get grass. But what was very gratifying, they informed us that a party of men from Oregon City, with provisions for our company had encamped with them, and were then at their camp. We hastened down the mountain, and in a few hours arrived at the camp. But imagine our feelings when we learned that those having provisions for us, had despaired of finding us, and having already been out longer than was expected, had returned to the settlement, carrying with them all the provisions, save what they had distributed to these men. We were wet, cold, and hungry, and would not be likely to overtake them. We prevailed upon one of the men whom we found at the camp, to mount one of our horses, and follow them. He was absent about ten minutes, when he returned and informed us that they were coming. They soon made their appearance. This revived us, and for awhile we forgot that we were wet and cold. * * *

"October 19.—After breakfast, the drovers left us; and as the party which had brought us provisions had been longer out than had been contemplated, Mr. Stewart and Mr. Gilmore wished to return. It was determined that Mr. Ruffner, the two females, Mr. Stewart, and Mr. N. Gilmore, should go on to the settlement, and that Mr. C. Gilmore, and the Indian who had been sent along to assist in driving the horses, and myself, should hasten on with the provisions to the camp. We were soon on the way, and climbing up the mountain. The horses were heavily loaded, and in many places the mountain was very slippery, and of course we had great difficulty in getting along. It was still raining heavily, and the fog so thick that a person could not see more than fifteen feet around. We traveled about two miles up the mountain, when we found that whilst it had been raining in the valley it had been snowing on the mountain. The trail was so covered with snow that it was difficult to find it, and, to increase our difficulty, the Indian refused to go any farther. We showed him the whip, which increased his speed a little, but he soon forgot it, was very sulky, and would not assist in driving. * * * When we ascended the hill to the eastern side of the gulf, we found the snow much deeper than upon the western side; besides, it had drifted, and rendered the passage over the strip of the old snow somewhat dangerous, as in many places the action of the water had melted the snow upon the under side and left a thin shell over the surface, and in some places holes had melted through. We were in danger of falling into one of these pits. Coming to one of these ravines where the snow had drifted very much, I dismounted in order to pick a trail through, but before this was completed, our horses started down the bank. I had discovered two of these pits, and ran to head the horses and turn them; but my riding horse started to run and went directly between the two pits; his weight jarred the crust loose, and it fell in, presenting a chasm of some twenty-five or thirty feet in depth, but the horse, being upon the run, made his way across the pit. The other horses, hearing the noise and seeing the pits before them, turned higher up, where the snow and ice were thicker, and all reached the opposite side in safety.

"Our Indian friend now stopped, and endeavored to turn the horses back, but two to one was an uneven game, and it was played to his disadvantage. He wanted an additional blanket; this I promised him, and he consented to go on. We soon met two Indians, on their way from The Dalles to Oregon City; our Indian conversed with them awhile, and then informed us of his intention to re-

THE FALLS OF MULTNOMAH AT THE CLOSE OF MIDSUMMER'S DAY.
The clear mountain torrent makes its last great leap from a vertical wall six hundred and seven feet above the
Columbia River Highway. If the Washington Monument stood in the pool above the Lower Falls, the
top of the Monument would barely reach to the top of the Upper Falls. The falling water is
broken into fine spray, and on a summer afternoon in June, before "Night draws
her sable curtain," the sun paints a rainbow for enchantment.

REINFORCED CONCRETE VIADUCT, COLUMBIA RIVER HIGHWAY.

This construction is unique. The steep slope of the mountain side at this point is composed of loose material, lying at the least angle of repose. In order not to disturb this rocky slope and start it rolling downward, this structure was designed, and it has served the purpose admirably. The surface of the road is twenty-two feet above the railway and the concrete railing is ten feet six inches from the center of the track.

turn with them. Whilst parleying with him, a party of men from our camp came up the mountain with their cattle; they had driven their teams to the small branch of the Deshutes, twelve miles below the mountain, where they had left the families, and started out with their cattle before the stream should get too high to cross. Whilst we were conversing with these men, our Indian had succeeded in getting one loose horse, and the one which he was riding, so far from the band of pack-horses that, in the fog, we could not see him, and he returned to the settlement with the two Indians we had just met.

"Our horses were very troublesome to drive, as they had ate nothing for thirty-six hours; but we succeeded in getting them over the snow, and down to the grassy ridge, where we stopped for the night. My friend Gilmore shouldered a bag of flour, carried it half a mile down the mountain to a running branch, opened the sack, poured in water, and mixed up bread. In the mean time, I had built a fire. We wrapped the dough around sticks and baked it before the fire, heated water in our tin cups and made a good dish of tea, and passed a very comfortable night. It had ceased raining before sunset, and the morning was clear and pleasant; we forgot the past, and looked forward to a bright future.

"October 20.—At 8 o'clock we packed up, took the trail down the mountain to the gravelly bottom, and then down the creek to the wagon-camp, which we reached at 3 P. M.; and if we had not before forgotten our troubles, we certainly should have done so upon arriving at camp. Several families were entirely out of provisions, others were nearly so, and all were expecting to rely upon their poor famished cattle. True, this would have prevented starvation; but it would have been meagre diet, and there was no certainty of having cattle long, as there was but little grass. A happier set of beings I never saw, and the thanks bestowed upon us by these families would have compensated for no little toil and hardship. They were supplied with an amount of provisions sufficient to last them until they could reach the settlements. After waiting one day, Mr. Gilmore left the camp for the settlement, taking with him three families; others started about the same time, and in a few days all but three families had departed. These were Mr. Barham's, Mr. Rector's, and Mr.

Caplinger's, all of whom had gone on to the settlement for horses. Ten men yet remained at camp, and, after selecting a suitable place for our wagon-yard, we erected a cabin for the use of those who were to remain through the winter, and to stow away such of our effects as we could not pack out. This being done, nothing remained but to await the return of those who had gone for pack horses. We improved the time in hunting and gathering berries, until the 25th, when four of us, loaded with heavy packs, started on foot for the valley of the Willamette.

"But before entering upon this trip, I will state by what means the timely assistance afforded us in the way of provisions was effected. The first party starting for the settlement from The Dalles, after we had determined to take the mountain route, carried the news to Oregon City that we were attempting a passage across the Cascade mountains, and that we should need provisions. The good people of that place immediately raised by donation about eleven hundred pounds of flour, over one hundred pounds of sugar, some tea, &c., hired horses, and the Messrs. Gilmore and Mr. Stewart volunteered to bring these articles to us. The only expense we were asked to defray was the hire of the horses. They belonged to an Indian chief, and of course he had to be paid. The hire was about forty dollars, which brought the flour to about four dollars per hundred, as t h e r e were about one thousand pounds when they arrived. Those who had the means paid at once, and those who were unable to pay gave their due bills. Many of the families constructed pack - saddles and put them on oxen, and, in one instance, a feather bed was rolled up and put  on an ox; but the animal did not seem to like his load, and ran into the woods, scattering the feathers in every direction; he was finally secured, but not until the bed was ruined. In most cases, the oxen performed well.

"In the afternoon of the 25th of October, accompanied by Messrs. Creighton, Farwell, and Buckley, I again started to the valley. We had traveled but a short dis-

THE WARM GLOW OF SUNSET AT THE CLOSE OF AN AUTUMN DAY.

Photo in color showing East viaduct of the Columbia River Highway near Multnomah Falls, October, 1914, before the paving was done. The sun burst through the clouds and produced color so bright that it seemed almost unreal. The long shadows cast by camera and men witness the late hour of the day. Curiosity caused the man behind to look at the camera when the picture was made, and it appears as if two heads were on one body.

COLUMBIA RIVER HIGHWAY, NEAR ONEONTA.

The mountains rise abruptly at this point, and the highway construction was difficult. The road-way is located on the side of the mountain 140 feet above the railroad tracks which skirt the south shore of the broad Columbia. In forming the shelf for the highway it was necessary to carry all of the waste material on tram cars for a considerable distance in each direction, in order not to interfere with the operation of trains immediately below.

tance when we met Barham and Rector, who had been to the settlement. They had some horses, and expected others in a short time. They had induced a few families whom they met near Mount Hood to return with them, and try their chance back to The Dalles; but, after waiting one day, they concluded to try the mountain trip again. We traveled up the bottom to the trail, where we encamped; about this time, it commenced raining, which continued through the night.

"October 26.—This morning at eight o'clock, we were on the way. It was rainy, and disagreeable traveling. We followed the trail over the main part of the mountain, when we overtook several families, who had left us on the twenty-second. Two of the families had encamped the night before in the bottom of the deep ravine; night overtook them, and they were compelled to camp, without fuel, or grass for cattle or horses. Water they had in plenty, for it was pouring down upon them all the night. One of their horses broke loose, and getting to the provision sack, destroyed the whole contents. There were nine persons in the two families, four of them small children, and it was about eighty miles to the nearest settlement. The children, as well as the grown people, were nearly barefoot, and poorly clad. Their names were Powell and Senters. Another family by the name of Hood, had succeeded in getting up the gravelly hill, and finding grass for their animals, and a little fuel, had shared their scanty supply with these two families, and when we overtook them they were all encamped near each other. We gave them about half of our provisions, and encamped near them. Mr. Hood kindly furnished us with a wagon cover, with which we constructed a tent, under which we rested for the night.

"October 27.—The two families who had lost their provisions succeeded in finding a heifer that belonged to one of the companies traveling in advance of us. In rambling upon the rocky cliffs above the trail for grass, it had fallen down the ledge, and was so crippled as not to be able to travel. The owners had left it, and as the animal was in good condition, it was slaughtered and the meat cured.

"After traveling four miles through the fresh snow, (which had fallen about four inches deep during the night,) we came to where the trail turned down to the Sandy. We were glad to get out of the snow, as we wore moccasins, and the bottoms being worn off, our feet were exposed. Two miles brought us to where we left the Sandy, and near the place where we met the party with provisions; here we met Mr. Ruffner, Mr. Lock, and a Mr. Smith, with fourteen pack-horses, going for effects to Fort Deposit—the name which we had given our wagon camp.

"The numerous herds of cattle which had passed along had so ate up the grass and bushes, that it was with great difficulty the horses could procure a sufficiency to sustain life. Among the rest, was a horse for me; and as I had a few articles at the fort, Mr. Ruffner was to take the horse along and pack them out. Two of his horses were so starved as to be unable to climb the mountains, and we took them back with us. The weather by this time had cleared up; we separated, and each party took its way.

"A short distance below this, our trail united with one which starting from The Dalles, runs north of Mount Hood, and until this season was the only trail traveled by the whites. We proceeded down the Sandy, crossing it several times, through thickets of spruce and alder, until we arrived at the forks, which were about fifteen miles from the base of Mount Hood."

Almost exhausted this company of pioneer home-builders struggled on down Sandy River, crossing a low ridge, and coming into the Clackamas Valley, which they followed to its junction with the Willamette, and on to Oregon City.

Only those who have climbed great mountains, and know the rugged slopes of Mount Hood and its glaciers, are able to appreciate in some small measure the terrible difficulties surmounted by those brave people.

Our mountaineers—"Mazamas", and members of kindred organizations throughout the world, have shown endurance, and performed great feats in mountain climbing, when properly shod—with hob-nailed, steel-calked boots, and with life line and Alpen-stock in hand, but Joel Palmer, the pioneer, outdid them all, when he climbed about the great snow-dome of Mount Hood; his moccasins gone, his calloused feet treading the sharp rocks and the ice of the glaciers, hewing steps out of the ice as he climbed higher

BEACON ROCK AND FISH WHEEL, FROM COLUMBIA RIVER HIGHWAY.

Beacon Rock (so called by Lewis and Clark) has always been a beacon to those who used this broad river. The ocean tides affect the flow of the river up to this point. Here the first Columbia River fish wheel was built by W. R. McCord, at the mouth of the creek of that name. The fourteen thousand acres set aside by the National Government as a public playground begins at this point.

SAINT PETER'S DOME, COLUMBIA RIVER HIGHWAY.

This mighty monolith is one of several, that stand like sentinels in the Gorge of the Columbia. The clouds play "hide and seek" around their heads, and the eagles make their nests among the crags. Every one who drives over the broad highway passes near the base of these towers of strength, that have withstood the centuries.

and higher, in order to see if some way was not open for his people to enter this land of promise.

Only once on this trip was he "alarmed", although food was exhausted, and he traveled down the mountain on the jump with an empty stomach and "at least 25 miles to travel before reaching those working on the road." This once was when he saw some deep ravines and crevasses in the ice, over which he must pass, as he descended the glacier and crossed its lower extremity above the canyon three thousand feet below.

Joel Palmer blazed the way for others to follow. The trail was widened, and became the Barlow Road of today. A franchise was granted by the Provisional Government to S. K. Barlow in 1846, and in 1848 this franchise was extended and the collection of tolls was authorized.

Such is the history of the first wagon road across the mountains in the Oregon country. The grades were steep, and in many places ropes were used to lower the wagons over the sides of the mountains. Some of the trees still show where the ropes wore away the bark when lines were wound around them to facilitate the lowering of the wagons. Some of these marks are twenty feet above the ground, showing that pioneers crossed these mountains on heavy snow late in the winter or early in the spring. If no rope was available, they would chop down a tree, and fasten the butt of it to the rear axle and drag it down the mountain behind them as a brake.

The Barlow Road has been improved from time to time and although narrow and the grades still steep, it is now possible to drive an automobile from Portland to the summit and across the range.*

After the establishment of a Provisional Government, May 2nd, 1843, an increasing number of emigrants poured into the Oregon Country.

*Several machines have gone over the mountains this year on the Barlow Road. Mr. George H. Himes, of the Oregon Historical Society, now seventy-two years young, a pioneer of '53, encircled the great snow peak of Mount Hood in an automobile, a little less than seventy years after Joel Palmer led the first emigrant train over the Cascade Mountains.

Mr. Himes started from Portland at 3:15 p. m., July 3rd, 1915, in a five passenger Michigan car. The party crossed the summit, and slept at Frog Lake, fifteen miles east of Government Camp. At 2:10 the next morning Mr. Himes was up. He strolled along the shores of the mountain lake, walking among wild flowers while communing with his God, and enjoying the dreamlike vision of Mount

Hood by moonlight. The great white pyramid seemed to touch the stars which sparkled like diamonds in the blue of the firmament, just preceding the dawn of a perfect day. The still waters mirrored the sky, the stars and the mountain. It was divinely beautiful, and as he looked, his blood ran free and his heart beat as full as it did in the days of his youth, and he thanked God for permitting him to live so long in this good land.

GEORGE H. HIMES

The party descended into the wheat fields of Eastern Oregon and returned to Portland in the afternoon through the gorge of the Columbia, over the newly constructed Columbia River Highway, arriving at 7:30 p. m., covering a distance of two hundred and twenty-four miles in a traveling time of fifteen hours.

Twenty-eight hours and fifteen minutes were spent in making the round trip; halting for sleep and refreshment, and occasionally for a look at the great snow domes of Mounts Rainier, Hood, Adams, St. Helens and Jefferson, and for short visits with friends.

Fractional currency was very scarce, and how to do business and effect exchange without it was a problem. The time was fast coming when sea shells and the highly colored beads* used by the Indians and the fur traders would have to give way to the coinage of metals.† The first Governor of Oregon Territory, George Abernethy, had a store at Oregon City. He lacked fractional currency, and in order to meet the situation, he induced the Indians to gather flat, rectangular pieces of flint rock from the place where they made their arrow points. He glued a

piece of tough paper around each stone, and wrote thereon his name, the year, and the amount which it would be good for at his store. When a customer carried a number of them he certainly had a "pocket full of rocks," and this is said to be the origin of that term.‡

In those early days the natural obstacles everywhere to be overcome were great, all means of transportation were crude and the burdens laid on the people by the transportation companies of that day were heavy.

*See Appendix E. Indian Beads and Mediums of Exchange. Gambling.
†See Appendix F. Coinage of gold into "Beaver Money."
‡Oregon Native Son.

EARLY MORNING AT EAGLE CREEK LOOKING TOWARD BONNEVILLE.

Color photograph made when work on the Highway was begun at this point September, 1914. Here the Columbia River Highway is blasted out of solid rock, and hangs on the side of the mountain, 200 feet above the great river, where the water surges around both sides of Bradford Island, at the foot of the rapids, below the Cascades.

THE COLUMBIA RIVER HIGHWAY IN THE HEART OF THE CASCADE RANGE.

Here the broad thoroughfare, twenty-four feet in width, was blasted out of solid rock. It is hung on the face of the cliff two hundred feet above the river. This photograph of the finished roadway was made only twelve months after the one in color, (page 87), which was made when the brush was being burned at this point.

PROGRESS OF A LIFETIME IN THE OREGON COUNTRY*

Transportation on the Columbia

The changes which have come within a life time, in methods of transportation along this great river are amazing. The high beaked Indian canoes, manned by naked savages; the rafts of logs on which the pioneers placed their "prairie schooners", to effect the passage of the gorge when their oxen could draw them no further over impossible Indian trails, are now but a remembrance of former days.

All of the physical obstructions to navigation have been removed as far inland as Lewiston, Idaho, a distance of five hundred miles. Today the traveling public hastens to and fro on swiftly moving trains on both sides of the great river. Passengers and merchandise are quickly conveyed across the continent, and only a few days are needed to negotiate distances which formerly required weeks or months of tireless labor.

The prices now charged by our common carriers for superior service, are but a fractional part of those of pioneer days. There is no longer a monopoly. The "Open River" and keen competition have changed the rule, and traffic is no longer taxed with all that it can bear.

The steamer "Lot Whitcomb" was launched on Christmas day, 1850. This was the beginning of an enterprise

---

*Mr. George H. Himes, who stands beside the great locomotive, (the second figure to the right) is a pioneer of '53. He came into the Oregon Country by ox team before the diminutive "Oregon Pony" locomotive was built. The relative size weight and capacity of two engines follow:

OREGON PONY	O. W.-R. & N. PASSENGER ENGINE No. 3225
Size of cylinders.....6 inches diameter	Size of cylinders....25 inches diameter
Size of drive wheels..34 inches diameter	Size of drive wheels..77 inches diameter
Weight of engine and tender....... ....9,700 pounds	Weight of engine and tender....... ....414,240 pounds
Will haul on a straight, level track at a speed of ten miles per hour ....219 tons	Will haul on a straight, level track at a speed of ten miles per hour ....10,442 tons

The modern locomotive weighs 42.7 times as much as the "Oregon Pony" and is 47.7 times as powerful.

(The Oregon Steam Navigation Company) which laid the foundation for many of the largest fortunes in the City of Portland.

At first the business was limited, but with the rapid development of the country it grew to immense proportions.

The Idaho gold excitement attracted thousands of miners, who went in by river. The Florence gold discovery of 1862 caused a flood of travel through the gorge of the Columbia.

The passage from Portland to The Dalles was eight dollars, and seventy-five cents extra for meals; Portland to Lewiston, sixty dollars, and meals and beds one dollar each.*

There was a portage on both sides of the river around the Cascades. The first one, built by the Bradfords, was on the Washington side. Early in May, 1853, Theodore Winthrop passed up the Columbia. He mentions the portage in writing to his mother from the "Dalles of the Columbia", May 10, '53. He said, "We left Vancouver on Monday in the little steamer Multnomah. At 4 P. M. we reached the landing at the foot of the rapids in the midst of the Cascade Mountains. These mountains are of the trap formation and present bold broken crags and precipitous fronts. The scenery has already been grander and wilder than any river I had seen† and upward to this place it became more and more singular and striking. The mountains are from 1,500 to 5,000 feet high, and the great river forces its way through them in a wild pine-clad gorge for sixty miles. We encamped at the landing, and next day took the luggage of the party up to the foot of the principal rapid in small boats, where we portaged on a rude tram road. The company being large,—Captain Brent's party, with one hundred days' provisions, and Capt. Wallen's company of infantry with baggage, ammunition, caissons, etc., etc.,—this process occupied two entire days, till we got on board a flat boat."‡

*Oregon Historical Society, Sept., 1908, "Oregon's First Monopoly."

†Theodore Winthrop had recently returned from a four year sojourn in Continental Europe.

‡"The Canoe and the Saddle," by Theodore Winthrop. Edited by Jno. H. Williams.

THE SOUTH PIER OF THE FABLED "BRIDGE OF THE GODS," LOOKING ACROSS EAGLE CREEK FROM THE COLUMBIA RIVER HIGHWAY. There is a beauty in the bare angles of the rocks which look down from the heights, where His Fingers broke them. Here He rent and tore them asunder, to make room for one of earth's great rivers.

EAGLE CREEK, COLUMBIA RIVER HIGHWAY.

This rustic arch of stone and concrete spans a clear mountain stream. It is sixty feet in length and harmonizes with the landscape. The waters of Eagle Creek are gathered from numerous mountain torrents which leap down from the summit of the Cascade Range, falling almost to the level of the sea in a distance of four miles. This bridge is at the base of "The South Pier of the Fabled Bridge of the Gods." See page 91.

Bradford's tramway was then in use between what was known as the Middle Landing and the upper Cascades on the Washington side.

As traffic increased Bradford was unable to handle the business and J. S. Ruckle built a wooden tramway on the Oregon side the whole length of the portage, the lower half, or from the Middle Landing down to a point just east of Bonneville, was of iron strap and over this portion of the road he ran a small engine. The cars on the upper part of the road were hauled by mules; as they were on the Bradford road on the Washington side.

There was an understanding and a business agreement between the two companies operating these tramways. As business increased the Ruckle's road on the Oregon side was improved, and the small steam engine ran the entire distance of some six miles between Bonneville and Cascade locks.

During the high stages of water from May to August, the steamers were unable to reach the Middle Landing because of the swift current. Bradford was therefore cut off and Ruckle got all the business, for which he received one-half the through freight charges from Portland to The Dalles. By this time the business was very great; the amount of freight for the new mining country was so large, that at times the whole portage at the Cascades was lined with freight from one end to the other. The losses resulting from thieving and damage were heavy, and as much as ten thousand dollars was paid in one month to shippers for losses thus sustained.

Great shipments of treasure passed over these portages and went out through Portland by steamship. On June 25th, 1861, this treasure was valued at $228,000.00; July 3rd, $50,000.00; August 12th, $20,000.00; August 24th, $195,558.00; September 12th, $130,000.00; September 30th, $315,780.00; October 3rd, $203,835.00; November 14th, $260,483.00; November 29th, $240,000.00; and on December 5th, $750,000.00. The little locomotive used on the Oregon side was called the "Oregon Pony." It was the first locomotive ever run, over the first railroad ever built, in the great state of Oregon. It was built in 1862 by the Vulcan Iron Works, of San Francisco, for use on the Ruckle portage road. It was shipped to Portland on the steamer Pacific, which was driven far north by a gale. The engine was, however, landed safely and was placed on a barge built especially to serve as a wharf boat and towed up the Columbia from Portland to Bonneville. This engine ran back and forth between the Cascade Locks and Bonneville for two years and earned many times its weight in gold during that short period. Every day it pulled an average of 200 tons of freight between Bonneville and the Cascades, though never a great deal going the other way, save twice a week when it would take down from five hundred to two thousand pounds of freight in shipments of gold from the Idaho mines. Although Bradford had agreed with Ruckle to "stand pat" on freight charges, which they fixed arbitrarily on all freight hauled by the steamboat companies, Bradford wavered when he saw the bulk of the business go to Ruckle on the Oregon side of the river.

J. C. Ainsworth was now president of the newly organized Oregon Steam Navigation Company, which absorbed the Dalles-Celilo portage and invested $100,000.00 in stocking the wagon road with teams and wagons. This immense caravan was soon taxed to its utmost, as was every thing else that the company owned. J. C. Ainsworth was dispatched to San Francisco. He found about twenty miles of railroad iron, which could be had by paying freight and other charges. He arranged to take all of the iron, as they would not divide the lot. Only fourteen miles of steel rails were needed for the Dalles-Celilo Portage Railroad, thus leaving enough for the Cascade Portage. When about three miles of rail had been laid at the Dalles Portage, Bradford grew uneasy at the continued success of Ruckle on the Oregon shores and sold out to the Oregon Steam Navigation Company for $155,000.00. This move put Ruckle and the "Oregon Pony" out of business. The little engine was sent to the Dalles-Celilo Portage for a short time, then it was sold to Mr. Howes, of San Francisco, and used in grading work, reducing the hills; on the site of one of which the Palace Hotel now stands. For nearly 20 years this little engine was safely stored; the warehouse burned and it was in a sad plight, until when it was overhauled and exhibited in Portland at the Lewis and Clark Exposition in 1905.

In the sixties it puffed and tugged away, passing along in the shadow of the great rock which overhangs the track and marks the divide in the Cascade Range. The rock

TABLE MOUNTAIN, THE NORTH PIER OF THE FABLED "BRIDGE OF THE GODS."

Looking across the great Columbia River from the Highway, Table Mountain is seen three thousand four hundred and twenty feet in height; its vertical walls show that it was broken off by some tremendous force. God did it in His own way, no doubt before man came. The tiny efforts of human beings seem as nothing beside the forces that tore this mountain range asunder.

COLUMBIA RIVER HIGHWAY AT EAGLE CREEK.

The finished roadway crosses the stream on an arch of stone and concrete. Substantial stone walls with concrete copings protect the traveling public. At right angles to the roadway, similar walls were built around the top of a large rock which extends out into the stream affording an excellent view of the landscape round about.

is still there, but instead of wooden rails on which strap irons were spiked for a distance of less than six miles, there are now two continuous rails of heavy steel reaching from Portland to Chicago, and parlor cars cover the distance in just seventy-two hours. A broad highway with easy grades and graceful curves now encircles the top of the rock and passes on through the mountain range. It is paved, and heavy stone and concrete walls protect the traveling public from danger as they look on the beautiful scenes. There is just enough room on the top of that rock to build a little stone house with plate glass windows and a green tile roof. There the "Oregon Pony" should have a resting place, and those who come and go, riding on cushioned seats and rubber tires may stop and think on the progress made in the Oregon Country in the short space of a man's lifetime; and who shall prophesy what shall come in the future, if one is able to judge by what has been accomplished in the past?

The Lion of Lucerne, designed by the great Thorwaldsen, is known to many millions of men and women who have journeyed far to see it. Placed on top of this rock, which marks the divide in a great range of mountains, the "Oregon Pony" will look down on strange scenes and attract all who come to the Pacific Coast of North America.

THE DIVIDE IN THE CASCADE RANGE

The little house on top of the rock is sketched in. It shows where the "Oregon Pony" will rest beside the Columbia River Highway, above the main line tracks of the O.-W. R. & N. Co.

The Columbia River Highway

ITH the rapid development of the Oregon Country there came a demand for a means of easy wagon communication, between the great "Inland Empire" east of the Cascade Range and the Willamette Valley, Puget Sound and the lower Columbia basin. It soon became an actual necessity.

A letter written by General Rufus Ingalls in 1864* tells a most interesting story, from a military standpoint:

"Headquarters Army of the Potomac,
Office Chief Quartermaster,

Camp near Brandy Station,
Hon. J. W. Nesmith,   March 23, 1864.
U. S. Senator, Washington.
Sir:
Having served as quartermaster on the Columbia River at (Fort) Vancouver for many years, and having had to

*The Quarterly of the Oregon Historical Society, June, 1914.

The broad thoroughfare is blasted out of the side of the mountain where it passes through the divide in the Cascade range. It curves around the rock two hundred feet above the main line tracks of the O.-W. R & N. Railway, where the "Oregon Pony" used to run over wooden rails, which were overlaid with strap iron. Starting below the rapids at the point seen in the upper right hand corner of the picture, it ran along the exact lines of the present tracks to Cascade Locks.

AUTUMN IN THE CASCADES NEAR BONNEVILLE.

Color photograph made September, 1914, before the road was paved. The rich colorings of the forest harmonize with the purple of the distant mountains, lending a charm to the ever-changing landscape all along the way.

FINISHED ROADWAY NEAR CROWN POINT, COLUMBIA RIVER HIGHWAY.

This is the western entrance to the Gorge of the Columbia. The grandeur of this scene is not surpassed. Travelers look down to the Columbia River 900 feet below, and they can also see the snow-capped peaks of the Cascade Range beyond, in the State of Washington.

supply the troops at the Cascades, Forts Dalles and Walla Walla, and to fit out and supply many military expeditions against the Indians east of the Cascades, I have always felt deeply impressed with the necessity of having a good wagon road from Vancouver to The Dalles, probably passing the Cascade Mountains on the Oregon side of the Columbia.

There are many cogent reasons for such a road aside from those of economy.

In 1849 and 1850 the troops east of the Cascades were supplied by means of bateaus manned by Indians. It was necessary to send provisions, forage, hospital and ordnance supplies up the river 50 miles, then to make a difficult, laborious and expensive portage of four or five miles at the Cascades, and then to reship and forward by boats to The Dalles.

These supplies had to be sent before the cold and rough weather of winter. Frequently in winter season, navigation is interrupted below the Cascades, when there can be no communication with the now populous and important country east without great risk.

I have known all communication with The Dalles to be cut off for weeks by extreme cold weather.

If a good wagon road were constructed, it would be used the year through to great advantage. I do not know what the rates of freight and passengers now are from Portland and Vancouver to The Dalles, but in 1858 and 1859 freight was $25 per ton and passage of horse or man, $10. When the Columbia River is closed by ice, of course there is no communication at all, as no practicable wagon road has ever been opened. Much public money has been disbursed for the transportation of troops and supplies on boats that might have been saved had there been an easy land route.

So soon as I can look over my books, I will furnish you a detailed statement showing the heavy and expensive shipments by the river to The Dalles. It amounted to more than $25,000 each quarter, and sometimes probably more than that sum in one month, dependent, of course, upon the season of the year and the forces east of the mountains. I refer to the amounts paid by Government for military purposes.

The country east of the Cascade Mountains is now quite populous and exceedingly rich in mineral and other resources. The trade by the river is now greater than at any other period, and is increasing.

The demand for a land route through the Cascade Mountains becomes more serious and important every day. As a military measure, it is important to connect the lower Columbia with the great interior by a practicable wagon road. I have seen the importance of it during the Indian wars. It would be still more necessary in case of a foreign war.

Respectfully submitted,

RUFUS INGALLS,

Brig. Gen., Chf. Qr. Mr., Army Potomac."

From this letter of General Ingalls it will be seen how necessary it has been ever since civilized man came into the Oregon country, to have a permanent road constructed through the Cascade Range, connecting the "Inland Empire" with the sea coast.

The first wagon road on the Oregon side of the river was completed on February 9th, 1856. It was less than six miles in length and ran from Bonneville to the Cascade Locks, passing over the top of a point of rock. The Portage Railroad was built at the base of this rock, which is the divide in the Cascade Range. The pioneer wagon road climbed to an elevation of four hundred and twenty-five feet on very steep grades to get by this difficult point. The new Columbia River Highway, which has no grade heavier than five per cent, passes around this point above the railroad, and below the old wagon road, at an elevation of two hundred and forty-five feet.

Although diligent search was made, no record could be found that would show exactly who built this first road. A news item in the "Oregonian" of February 9th, 1856, reads: "We are informed that a new road around the portage of the Cascades, on the Oregon side, has been completed and that goods are now being transported over this road with safety and dispatch." On the same date an article appeared in the "Oregonian" calling attention to the fact that W. R. Kilborn, who resided at the Lower Cascades, on the Oregon side, had perfected "arrangements for the transportation of freight over the portage

THE STATE FISH HATCHERY AT BONNEVILLE ON THE COLUMBIA RIVER HIGHWAY.

Bonneville is in the heart of the Cascade Range. The country is wild and will always be so, for the mountains are rugged and the streams which come down from great heights cut many a gorge in which wild game and fish abound. The fourteen thousand acres of Government land recently set aside for public recreation in this vicinity is now open to all. The fish hatchery is one of the largest in the world.

A MAGNIFICENT VIEW POINT, COLUMBIA RIVER HIGHWAY.

The curving road winds around the steep sides of the mountain on easy grades. There is always a good sight ahead and everywhere the traveler is protected from danger by strong walls of stone and concrete.

at the Cascades on the Oregon side." Continuing, Mr. Kilborn said, "The road is now in complete order and my teams will always be in readiness."

The records in the United States Land Office at Portland show this road to have been in existence in 1859, just as it now is.

Although the question was frequently agitated, and there was great need of a through road, no definite action was taken until October 23, 1872, when the State Legislature of Oregon appropriated fifty thousand dollars for

A PACIFIC COAST "CORNICHE."

The road is blasted out of solid rock for several miles and there are two and a half miles of dry masonry walls of this character in Multnomah County; an average height of eleven and a half feet.

the purpose of building a wagon road from the mouth of Sandy River in Multnomah County, through the gorge of the Columbia to The Dalles. This amount was expended, and in October, 1876, an additional appropriation of fifty thousand dollars was provided. The road built was crooked and narrow, and the grades were steep. In constructing the O. W. R. & N. Railway through the gorge of the Columbia in 1883, this road was destroyed in many places, and only traces of it could be found in 1913, when construction was begun on the new Columbia

River Highway, twenty-four feet in width; with no grade heavier than five per cent.

Previous to this, on March 25th, 1910, Mr. Henry Wemme and others, petitioned the authorities of Multnomah County, to construct a road from the town of Bridal Veil, east to the Hood River County line. The official road viewers made a favorable report. The county surveyor ran a line from Bridal Veil to the eastern boundary of Multnomah County and made a map and profile which were filed. He also ran a line, starting

CROWN POINT.

The road encircles the top of the rock seven hundred and twenty-five feet above the river, and fits it like a crown. The concrete walk is seven feet in width. The protection railing is ornamented with concrete lamp posts twenty feet apart.

from a point near Chanticleer, and endeavored to locate a new road from that point to Latourell. This he said was impracticable and could not be done, even allowing a maximum grade of twelve per cent. The only road existing at that time between the last named points had grades as high as twenty-two per cent.

On April 29th, 1911, the report of the road viewers and the County Surveyor on the road between Bridal Veil and Hood River County's line was adopted, and shortly thereafter the County force constructed one and eight-tenths mile of road east of Bridal Veil, twenty feet in

MOUNT HOOD FROM THE VALLEY OF HOOD RIVER.

The completion of the Columbia River Highway makes the beautiful valley and the town of Hood River a suburb of Portland. In three hours' time one can have a complete change of climate; going from the soft salt air of the sea to the crisp dry air of Eastern Oregon. The Cascade Range has stood as a great rock wall between the "Inland Empire" and Western Oregon, but it has now been pierced by this Highway.

LOOKING WEST FROM MITCHELL POINT, COLUMBIA RIVER HIGHWAY.

Here the great river resembles a mountain lake although it is swift and turbulent, where it narrows at "Celilo," "The Dalles," "Cascade Locks" and other places. Many crystal streams cascade down the steep slopes of the mountains, falling from great heights, hence the name given by early travelers, "Cascade Mountains."

width, which conformed to the general practice of that time, with steep grades and short curves.

When the County construction force began to dig into the steep slopes of the mountain side above the main tracks of the O. W. R. & N. Company, the work was stopped until an agreement could be entered into between the Railway Company and the County authorities, permitting the joint use of their right-of-way at many points, where the rugged mountains made this necessary. This agreement provided that Multnomah County might build

A section of the new pavement, eighteen feet in width, on the Columbia River Highway. The rock shoulders were not completed when this photograph was made.

any width of roadway desired, but in no case more than fourteen feet in width, the grades to be seven and one-half per cent, although in many places a twelve-foot roadway had been contemplated, with grades as high as nine per cent. This much having been done all work ceased, for seemingly the Columbia River Highway had no supporters except a few "road enthusiasts."

Shell Rock Mountain, in Hood River County, had always been regarded as an impassable barrier. No wagons were able to get by this mountain in pioneer days; the hardy homeseekers used to stop just east of this point to cut down trees and make their rafts of logs on which they floated down the river to the Cascades. The road which the State built in the seventies crossed this rock slide far above the present road. The loose rock slopes were so steep that it was not possible to maintain the old road, and it soon fell into decay.

Had it not been for the timely assistance of one of Portland's prominent citizens, all work would have stopped for many years. In the fall of 1912, Mr. S. Benson placed ten thousand dollars in the hands of Governor Oswald West, to be used in connection with prison labor, in building a new road around the base of Shell Rock Mountain.

Tunnel and bridge at Oneonta Gorge— The rock is two hundred and five feet high. Only eighteen feet of rock was left between the railway tracks and the Columbia River Highway.

At this time the State of Oregon had no Highway Commission, and the work was undertaken by the authorities of Hood River County, who used the State prisoners; the expense being met from the funds provided by Mr. Benson.

This revived interest and created sentiment all along the line, favorable to the Columbia River Highway. It stimulated Multnomah County to action and called attention to the need of engineering skill and supervision, the lack of which had caused the work done by prison labor in Hood River County to fail, for most of the money contributed by Mr. Benson was wasted.

On July 26, 1913, the new Commissioner, Rufus C. Holman, Chairman of the County Board of Multnomah County, offered the following resolution, which was adopted:

"Whereas, under the provisions of Chapter One Hundred and Three of the laws of Oregon, Nineteen Thirteen, certain procedures are specified, and certain provisions designated relating to roads and highways, it is therefore,

CANNON BEACH—SOUTH OF TILLAMOOK HEAD.

Many years ago an old iron cannon of ancient mold was cast up on this beach, where it is now kept as a relic. This is one of the most picturesque parts of the shores of the broad Pacific Ocean. It is fully equal to any in the world. Above the moss-covered rocks, and fir-clad hills, is a range of high mountains whose purple tints make harmony with the green of the ocean and the musical waves, when they break into foam on these rocks, or gently curl over the white sands of the beach.

THREE-HINGED CONCRETE BRIDGE, MOFFETT CREEK, COLUMBIA RIVER HIGHWAY.

The curving lines of this arch are harmonious and pleasing. Its boldness is in keeping with the surrounding landscape. God made this country on a mighty scale. The mountains are high and the river is broad and deep. The towering rock, three miles distant on the north bank of the river, was a beacon to Lewis and Clark and the pioneer home-seekers who came after them.

"Resolved, That an Advisory Board on Roads and Highways to the Board of County Commissioners be created, consisting of Mr. W. W. Cotton, Mr. A. S. Benson, Mr. C. S. Jackson, Mr. W. B. Fechheimer and Mr. Samuel Hill, to investigate present conditions and methods prevailing in this department of County affairs, and to recommend those things which they may deem necessary for the betterment of the service."

On August 27th, 1913, the Advisory Board recommended the employment of a road expert and engineer

MOFFETT CREEK BRIDGE, COLUMBIA RIVER HIGHWAY.
This is the largest flat arch bridge in America and the largest three-hinged arch in the world. The clear span is one hundred and seventy feet and it rises only seventeen feet in that distance. The floor of the bridge is seventy feet above the stream.

to supervise the construction of the Columbia River Highway in Multnomah County. On August 28th, 1913, the Board of County Commissioners entered into an agreement with the author of this book to serve the Commission and the people of Multnomah County as Consulting Engineer.

A careful study of the great gorge of the Columbia, revealed its wonderful beauty and the great possibilities for a scenic and commercial highway. It was decided that the best modern practice should be followed in building a road suited to the times, the traffic, and the place. Such a road to have a minimum width of twenty-four feet, with extra width on all curves, and no radius less than one hundred feet. The maximum grade to be five per cent.

Early in September preliminary surveys were started, and the first construction camp was established at Multnomah Falls in October, 1913.

Interest in the Columbia River Highway increased rapidly. The daily press gave it their unanimous support. The Columbia Highway Association, with Mr. Julius Meier as its President, worked unceasingly to secure

THE DIVIDE IN THE CASCADE RANGE, LOOKING NORTH TOWARD TABLE
MOUNTAIN IN THE DISTANCE.

When Theodore Winthrop looked on the rugged scenery at this point in 1853, he said: "It will bear cultivation admirably; also: and sometime—a thousand years hence, the beauty of its highly finished shores will be exquisite."

its completion to the sea, while Mr. S. Benson and other influential citizens encouraged the people of Hood River County, and backed the whole enterprise. The same spirit of helpfulness which filled the breast of Joel Palmer and his comrades in the early days, when they came into the Oregon country, seemed now to urge men on to action.

The newly-created State Highway Commission was anxious to lend assistance and to have all the Counties act in unison in order that all of the work might conform as nearly as possible to one standard, and to avoid local limitations. It was, therefore, thought best to have Mult-

SUNSET FROM KING'S HEIGHTS OVERLOOKING THE CITY OF PORTLAND.

After God had fashioned the Gorge of the Columbia and fixed the course of the broad river, He planted a garden; men came and built a beautiful city close by this wonderland, in which they might dwell, and with contentment look upon the snow-capped mountains round about. Mount Hood in the distance is only one of five snow peaks that can be seen from Portland.

EASTWARD THROUGH THE GORGE OF THE COLUMBIA FROM CROWN POINT.

A magnificent panorama is revealed to all travelers who circle around the top of the great rock on the Columbia River Highway. The road is wide and the solid concrete walk and railing protect visitors, while they look on the mighty handiwork of God. Beacon Rock, which rises abruptly from the river, is seen in the distance. The snow capped mountains beyond are thirty-five miles away.

nomah County take the lead, in placing the surveys and location of the entire Highway from the Inland Empire to the sea, under the supervision of the State Highway Commission; the difficult work in Multnomah County being done under the direction of the Consulting Engineer, who revised all surveys and fixed all locations through the Columbia River gorge in Multnomah County.

As the Panama-Pacific Exposition was expected to attract large numbers of tourists to this Coast, the authorities determined if it were possible to do so, to have the entire road completed and opened to traffic by mid-summer of 1915.

In order to facilitate the work and to avoid the usual entanglements and delays incident to an enterprise of such magnitude, it was necessary to start the heavy construction in Multnomah County at once, and to push it vigorously. Therefore, it was decided to do the work by day labor, and to establish a number of large camps, if some reliable citizen could be found who would accept the newly-created office of Roadmaster in Multnomah County.

Mr. John B. Yeon, a wealthy and public-spirited citizen of Portland, volunteered to give, without remuneration, his entire time to this splendid work; and his offer was quickly accepted. Mr. Yeon's long experience in handling men in lumber camps fitted him admirably for this great task. His sagacity and love of the beautiful enabled him to grasp the meaning of the Engineer's plans, and thus to decide important matters correctly and with great dispatch.

With such an organization, strenuous effort, under any and all conditions of weather became a pleasure.

The work was completed on time, and early in the summer of 1915, contracts for paving the Columbia River Highway and all of the trunk roads of Multnomah County, amounting to One Million Two Hundred and Fifty Thousand Dollars were awarded.

The road was officially opened between Portland and Hood River on July 6th, 1915, when thousands of automobiles from almost every State in the Union began to use America's Great Highway through the Cascade Mountains to the sea; although the west end of the Columbia Highway was not officially opened until August 11th, when a large number of machines went over the road from Portland to Astoria and on to Gearhart and the ocean beaches.

The work done in Hood River County eliminates all steep and dangerous grades. The new construction is of the highest type, and the tunnel in the face of the cliff at Mitchell Point, with the concrete viaduct approaches,* may well be considered among the most wonderful pieces of highway construction in the civilized world. It is fully equal to the famous "Axenstrasse" of Switzerland and one of the great features of the Highway.

For the first time in history it is possible to drive a wagon from the wheat fields of Eastern Oregon through the Cascade Mountains to the sea, and to those who have always thought with Sir George Simpson that it could never be done, we paraphrase the answer of Doctor Marcus Whitman and say "There is a wagon road through these mountains, for we have made it." An automobile can cover the entire distance in one short day's travel, and no man can estimate the value of this great Highway to all the people of the Pacific Coast.

Men of all stations have vied with each other in their giving, to help along this work.

Mr. John B. Yeon contributed two years of active service, aided by his friend and neighbor, A. S. Benson.

At Crown Point approximately two acres were donated, through the kindness of Osmon Royal.

George Shepperd gave eleven acres for the good of his fellows. Simon Benson made it possible for thousands to enjoy a broad river, high mountains, and sparkling water falls, by his gift of more than three hundred acres.

Jacob Kanzler found a way for our National Government to assist by setting aside some fourteen thousand acres of the National Forest for the free use of all, in which tired men and women with their little children may enjoy the wild beauty of nature's art gallery, and recreate themselves.

Just two years ago there came together a small group of men, who were fully assured that the time was ripe for the inception of this great work. They set about the task with strong determination and brought it to pass; for

---

*This tunnel was located and constructed by J. A. Elliott, under Major H. L. Bowlby, the State Highway Engineer.

ROSES ARE EVERYWHERE IN PORTLAND, OREGON.

"All the world knows the Portland rose," and will soon know about the Columbia River Highway and John B. Yeon, a prominent citizen of Portland, Oregon, whose claim to love and respect is based upon his service to others. Mr. Yeon is giving more than two years of his valuable time to the construction of the Columbia River Highway, and the improvement of all the roads in Multnomah County. His car was in the floral parade of 1915.

THE TUNNEL OF MANY VISTAS, MITCHELL POINT—COLUMBIA RIVER HIGHWAY.

At Mitchell Point, the mountains are high; the precipitous cliffs extend almost to the water's edge, leaving just room enough for a railway track to pass between their base and the broad Columbia. In order to maintain an easy grade and go around the face of the cliff by the shortest route, it was necessary to bore this tunnel 100 feet above the railway track. (See pages 123-124.) This work will compare favorably with that of any road construction in all the world.

dreams will come true if the dreamers work without ceasing to accomplish a purpose, when the purpose is pure.

On the morning of August 11th, 1915, Mr. Julius Meier, President of the Columbia Highway Association, invited a small group of men to breakfast with him before starting to drive over the new Columbia River Highway from Portland to the sea. The occasion was a happy one and all remembrance of hard knocks, and bruises, received in the effort to accomplish something really worth while, were forgotten when Samuel Hill presented to John B. Yeon a beautiful gold-lined silver loving cup, which bore the following inscription:

To

JOHN B. YEON

Roadmaster, Citizen, Husband, Father, Friend;

Who seeking to serve others found a new happiness for himself. May others drink from this never failing cup and find the draft as sweet.

PORTLAND, ORE.,
August 11, 1915.

On the reverse side were engraved the names of the donors:

Amos S. Benson,
S. Benson,
H. L. Bowlby,
Samuel Hill,
Rufus C. Holman,
C. S. Jackson,
S. C. Lancaster,
Julius L. Meier,
Frank Terrace,
Oswald West,
John F. Carroll,
H. L. Pittock.

The way is now open, and as long as men and women continue to come and go through the gorge of the Columbia they will see the mighty work of God and should glorify His name.

ADDENDA
1-9-1-6

Although, for more than a hundred years, men have planned, and worked almost without ceasing, to secure the construction of a passable road through the Gorge of the Columbia, the dream was not realized until the summer of 1915, one hundred and ten years after Lewis and Clark with Indian guides in their canoes descended the river with the purpose of exploring the Oregon country. The rapidity with which this highway was constructed when the proper time had arrived has astonished everyone, and has challenged the admiration of all who have any knowledge of the time usually required for such execution. In less than two years from the date of starting the first surveys to fix the location of the Highway, the entire road could be traveled for a distance of almost two hundred miles.

When the European war started, those in charge of this great road realized that tourist travel was likely to be cut off from Continental Europe for several years. The Panama Pacific Exposition was attracting the attention of the world to the Pacific Coast, and these men knew that Oregon's opportunity was at hand; therefore all possible speed was made, in order to be able to take first place in America.

The citizens of Portland and the people of the counties bordering on the Columbia River, determined to construct the greatest Highway ever built to meet the conditions of modern traffic; for it must be understood that the new means of conveyance—high power automobiles and auto trucks—have revolutionized methods of road construction throughout the world in the last ten years.

When all plans had been fully completed, and practically all of the work of construction had been finished, the author's official connection with it was severed, but his affection and interest in the work will last throughout the remaining years of his life.

THE VIADUCT AND TUNNEL AT MITCHELL POINT ON THE COLUMBIA
RIVER HIGHWAY.

In the State of Oregon, the Cascade Mountains were always an impassable barrier until the Barlow Road (then but little more than a cattle trail) was opened in 1848, and crossed the Range south of Mount Hood on steep and dangerous grades.

Since that time, Railroads and Steamboats have been the only means of communication through the Columbia River Gorge until the completion of this great Highway in 1915.

The reinforced concrete Viaduct and Tunnel eliminate all heavy grades. The way is now open from the wheat fields of Eastern Oregon to the City of Portland and on to the Sea. The Viaduct is two hundred and eight feet long and the Highway is one hundred feet above the main line tracks of the O.-W. R. R. & N. Co.

The tunnel is three hundred and ninety feet in length and the five windows look out over the mile-wide Columbia to the lofty mountains—surpassing in beauty the German Rhine.

The Tunnel of Many Vistas, at Mitchell Point, on Columbia River Highway.

The famous Axenstrasse tunnel of Switzerland has three windows overlooking Lake Uri and the mountains round about.

This tunnel on the Columbia River Highway has five great windows looking out over the broad Columbia and the rugged peaks of the Cascade Range.

Paving

As no trunk road can serve its purpose without a hard and durable surface, the next important step was taken up, and the speed with which the paving was done is no less remarkable than that of the road construction.

Early in the Spring of 1915, a campaign was launched by Messrs. Benson and Yeon, for paving the Columbia River Highway in Multnomah County for a distance of forty-two and a half miles, from Portland, east through the Gorge of the Columbia, to the Hood River County line, and also for paving several other trunk roads, the estimated cost of which was one million, two hundred and fifty thousand dollars.

The Portland Chamber of Commerce and some of the foremost citizens of Portland and Multnomah County, participated in a whirlwind campaign. An election was ordered on March 16th, and held April 14th. The bonds carried overwhelmingly, were advertised, and were sold May the 12th, bringing a premium of twenty thousand, six hundred and twenty-five dollars. Bids for paving, embracing all of the standard types, were asked, and contracts were awarded June the 17th. The Columbia River Highway is now paved with Warrenite for its entire distance in Mult-nomah County. Almost sixty miles of paving was completed before the winter rains began in November, 1915, and it is now possible to drive an automobile over a paved roadway into the very heart of the Cascade Mountain Range from the City of Portland, through the Gorge of the Columbia, in less than two hours.

Preparedness

The road which, in 1864, General Rufus Ingalls saw the need of, is now a reality. Of it he said, "The demand for a land route through the Cascade Mountains becomes more serious and important every day. As a military measure, it is important to connect the lower Columbia with the great interior by a practicable wagon road. I have seen the importance of it during the Indian wars. It will be still more necessary in case of Foreign wars."

The people of the Oregon country have built this great highway for agricultural and commercial pursuits, as well as for the enjoyment of the beautiful and grand in nature. No thought was given to the military aspect; although, in the light of recent events, it is most important that our National Government should undertake the construction of permanent trunk roads throughout America, connecting all important centers with strategic points along our Coast and frontier lines.

At no time in the history of the world have roads played so important a part in the life of Nations as they do today. The splendid roads of France made it possible, in the most terrible war of all history, to utilize great numbers of power trucks, automobiles, taxi-cabs, motor-cycles, and other types of modern conveyance, for concentrating a large force quickly at a given point; preventing the downfall of Paris, and winning victory at the battle of the Marne.

In all parts of our country the question of preparedness is being freely discussed, and all patriots agree that we must be prepared to prevent the invasion of any part of this great land. A comprehensive system of permanent roads lies at the base of all preparedness, and this Nation should lose no time in constructing such a system of roads as quickly as possible.

TUNNEL AT ONEONTA GORGE AND FINISHED PAVEMENT, COLUMBIA
RIVER HIGHWAY.

At Oneonta Gorge the Columbia River Highway crosses the stream on a concrete bridge and enters a tunnel which pierces the east wall of the Gorge, which is two hundred and five feet in height.

In this picture the road is seen in the shadow of a great wall of rock, while the bridge is in the sunlight which shines through the deep narrow cleft in the side of the mountain, known as Oneonta Gorge. In the depths of this gorge there is a beautiful waterfall, three hundred feet in height. See page 41.

The combination of light and shadow makes a striking picture, and one that can never be forgotten.

The Larch Mountain Trail, Columbia River Highway

Larch Mountain has been called Nature's Grandstand, for such it appears to be in all reality. There is no better viewpoint from which to look on Nature's wondrous beauties as revealed in the rugged, tree-clad Cascade Range. From the summit of Larch Mountain the whole creation round about for many miles, is seen in all directions. Crest above crest, the dark green mountains rise to the north, to the south, and to the east, as if they were the bulking waves of a tremendous ocean driven by some titanic gale. Five "fire mountains which once blazed like beacons along the North Pacific Coast" can be seen at once, "their craters healed with snow" which never leaves them. Leaving the Columbia River Highway and starting up from either Multnomah or Wahkeena Falls, a safe and comfortable foot and pony trail winds to the summit of Larch Mountain, which has an elevation of 4045 feet. The distance by way of Multnomah Falls is six and one-half miles, and the distance from Multnomah to Wahkeena

Falls by this trail through Benson Park is four and one-half miles. (See pages 11-12-144.)

National Dedication of the Highway

Wednesday, June 7th, 1916, has been designated as the date for the formal dedication of the great thoroughfare which extends from the Pacific Ocean, through the Coast Range, through the Gorge of the Columbia in the Cascade Mountains, and on to the "Inland Empire." President Wilson, Members of Congress, and Representatives of all Foreign Nations have been invited to be present and to participate in this historic event. All arrangements having been perfected, the dedicatory exercises will be held at Multnomah Falls, and at Crown Point; with appropriate exercises in connection with the beginning of the construction of Vista House, the Pioneer Memorial to be erected in the center of the circular area, on top of the great rock overlooking the broad Columbia.

In the White House, at exactly 8 P. M., President Wilson will press an electric button which will close a circuit reaching across the Continent. This will operate an electric magnet on Crown Point at 5 P. M., Pacific Coast time, and cause a weight to drop which will unfurl our flag to the breezes of the Pacific Ocean and cause it to float from the mast erected on the site of the Memorial building. A National salute will then be fired.

Photographs will be made simultaneously of President Wilson pressing the electric button in the White House and of the unfurling of our flag and firing of the salute at Crown Point on the Pacific Coast. By this means the President will extend his hand across the Continent, thus reaching into the future and unfurling the flag of freedom three hours ahead of Washington time.

"Long may our land be bright with freedom's holy light." May we realize full soon that we must build a system of permanent National Highways, that will be suited to the times, the traffic, and the needs of each particular section, and of our country as a whole.

Efficiency and preparedness are demanded in this age. The times are pregnant. We cannot be efficient, nor can we be prepared to meet the issues of peace or war, until we have constructed a system of permanent roads connecting all important centers and strategic points.

"It is toward evening, and the day is far spent," let us work while we can for Our Country.

GOD'S GOOD-NIGHT KISS WHEN THE DAY IS DONE.

The beauties of the Gorge of the Columbia can never be forgotten. Returning to Portland at sunset on a perfect day, the visitor may pass through the busy streets, ascend to the heights, and as the shadows come and darkness fills the valley, look down upon the city, where myriads of lights are beginning to twinkle like jewels in a diadem. Up in the sky, as if "Of earth apart," is seen the snow-clad peak of Mount Hood.

The last rays of rose-colored sunlight give the good-night kiss to the mountains and the tired world below.

VISTA HOUSE AT CROWN POINT; A PIONEER MEMORIAL.

Upon the completion of the great highway, the people of the Oregon country determined to erect to the memory of the Pioneers, a permanent building on top of the great rock at Crown Point. This building is a tribute to the pioneers now living, as well as to those brave spirits who entered through the Columbia gateway, risked their lives that we might possess this good land, and have since gone to their homes on the other shore.

[130]

APPENDIX "A"
The "Bees Wax Ship"

CANDLES OF BEES WAX

Remains of Honey Bee

A ship was wrecked and went to pieces on the Oregon Coast long years ago, before any white man is known to have visited these shores. Undoubtedly a large part of her cargo was beeswax, for hundreds of tons of wax have been dug from the sands of the old sea beach, some distance back from the present shore line. Many large candles, some of them two inches in diameter, were found. In a few of them the wicks were still intact. No doubt they were intended for altar purposes, in some Spanish mission, in California or Mexico.

Where did so much beeswax come from? is the question which has often been asked. Some have thought it to be mineral wax, although the remains of a honey bee was found encased therein, and it has the smell and taste of beeswax. A large piece of this wax nearly two feet square, has Roman letters cut on its surface. This wax was found south of Cannon Beach. (See page 111.)

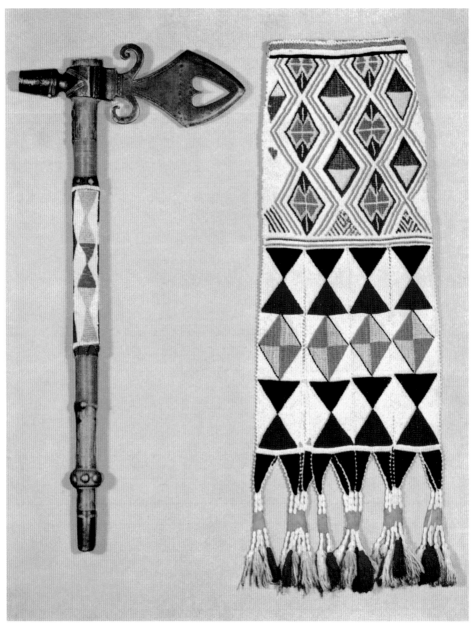

TOMAHAWK-PIPE AND TOBACCO POUCH.

This is the type of "Peace-pipe" used in the early days by the Hudson's Bay Company as a token of friendship. It was owned by Tom-A-Has, the Indian who killed Dr. Marcus Whitman in the massacre of 1847. These articles are now in the possession of the Oregon Historical Society, Portland, Oregon. They were photographed direct from the originals by the four color process. Reduced three and one-half diameters.

APPENDIX "B"

The Whitman Massacre

NOVEMBER, 1847

GROUP OF FOUR SURVIVORS.

PHOTO BY DAVIES

Mrs. Nancy Osborn Jacobs

Mrs. Elizabeth Sager Helm   Mrs. Helen M. Saunders Church   Mrs. Gertrude Hall Denny

Mrs. Jennie Christenson, the daughter of Mrs. Church, stands on the left.
Mrs. Marie Stratton, the daughter of Mrs. Helm, stands on the right.

The terrible massacre which occurred November 29-30, 1847, at the Whitman Mission, six miles west of the present city of Walla Walla, Washington, can never be forgotten.

Dr. Whitman and his sweet wife, together with twelve others, were massacred, and the buildings were burned, by the Cayuse Indians. More than fifty women and children were taken prisoners, but were rescued by Peter Skeen Ogden, Chief Factor of the Hudson's Bay Company at Fort Vancouver, and were taken to Oregon City early in January, 1848. On the 28th day of June, 1915, sixty-seven years after that horrible event, Mrs. Church, now in her eighty-first year, met three other survivors, whom she had not seen since she was a girl of fourteen, when they parted company at Oregon City.

The five Indians who led in the murderous attack on the Whitman Mission were captured. They were tried by a jury of twelve men; were convicted and hung at Oregon City on the third day of June, 1850.—*George H. Himes, of the Oregon Historical Society.*

When Lewis and Clark explored the Columbia River, they stopped at an Indian Lodge on the afternoon of October 17th, 1805.

The squaws were engaged in splitting and drying salmon. Clark says, "I was furnished with a mat to set on and one man set about preparing me something to eat; first he brought in a piece of Dried log of pine and with a wedge of elk's horn, and a mallet of Stone, curiously carved, he Split the log into Small pieces and laid it upon the fire on which he put round Stones. A woman handed him a basket of water and a large Salmon about half Dried; when the Stones were hot he put them into the basket of water with the fish, which

THE DIVIDE IN THE CASCADE RANGE OPPOSITE THE FOOT OF THE LOWER CASCADES OF THE COLUMBIA RIVER.

The "Oregon Pony" locomotive will be placed on top of the rock to the left, and a statute commemorating the struggle of the early pioneers, will stand on top of the rock to the right. Photograph was made just before the road was paved.

was soon sufficiently boiled for us; it was then taken up, put on a plate of rushes neetly made, and set before me. They boiled a Salmon for each of the men with me."*

The change that has come in the Oregon country in the short space of 110 years is truly marvelous. The opportunity which is offered to intelligent men at this time is even greater than it was in the early days.

Major General George W. Goethals, builder of the Panama Canal, passed over the Columbia River Highway between Portland and Cascade Locks on Wednesday, September 1st, 1915. He said, "The Columbia River Highway is a splendid job of engineering, and absolutely without equal in America for scenic interest."

---

*Clark was too busy observing what he saw (and he seems to have seen everything) to pay any attention to spelling, punctuation, or the use of capitals.

INDIAN BEADS AND OTHER ORNAMENTS.

Photographed direct by four-color process; one-half size. People of many races have mingled and trafficked for long years past, on the shores of the great Columbia. Oriental beads were brought in ships for the purpose of barter and exchange by fur traders. This collection was made in the vicinity of Memaloose Island (the Island of the Dead), not far from The Dalles, Oregon. They are known as Hudson's Bay beads.

FLATHEAD WOMAN AND CHILD.

Cow-Wacham was a fashionable woman of the Cowlitz Indian tribe. She lived on the shores of the Cowlitz River near its confluence with the Columbia. The picture is a fac-simile reproduction from a sketch made by Paul Kane in the year 1846. The painting was lithographed and printed in London in 1859, requiring six impressions in six different colors to produce.

Flathead Indians

All of the early explorers who came into the Oregon country, noticed that some of the Indians had flattened skulls. The custom can be traced to almost all the tribes of the lower Columbia as well as of the Willamette Valley and Puget Sound country, including Vancouver Island.

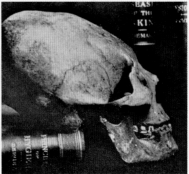

Flathead skull found near Maryhill in Klickitat County, Washington.

It was fashionable, and prevailed among the upper class. Slaves were not permitted to flatten the heads of their children.

On September 11, 1836, Mrs. Whitman saw an Indian mother at the Cascades with her infant. The child's head was in the "pressing machine," and Mrs. Whitman tells us that this horrible practice was continued until "the head became a fashionable shape."

A noted artist, Paul Kane, visited the Oregon country in 1845. He made many sketches and published a book entitled "Wanderings of An Artist Among the Indians of North America." His book was printed in London in 1859 and contained "seven illustrations printed in colors." They were lithographs, requiring six impressions to each picture.

Early in April, 1846, he sketched a "Flat-Head Woman and Child" (see opposite page) near the mouth of the Cowlitz river. Her name was "Cow-Wacham." Kane visited Puget Sound, and on his return, June 15 of the same year, he met a half-breed who told him that Cow-Wacham was dead, and that, because he had made a sketch of her, he was supposed to be the cause of her death. Kane lost no time in procuring a canoe and leaving for Fort Vancouver.

In 1912, the author met "Scoocoom," meaning the "Evil Genius," a chief of the Klickitat tribe, and inquired whether his people had ever resorted to the practice of flattening the skull. The fine looking old man said: "No, my mother—she lazy—your mother—she lazy too;" indicating that much care and patience were required on the part of mothers, in order to produce a fashionable skull.

The women of China worked on the other extremity of the body and compressed the feet of their girls, while "Godey's Lady Book" of 1857 shows that a middle course was pursued by the young women of America. They compressed the waist line to the limit of human endurance for fashion's sake. The time has now arrived when men and women need to have the full use of their heads, their feet, and every organ, in order to fulfill the requirements of this age and generation.

Indians and River Called Multnomah

Lewis and Clark called the Indians on Sauvie's Island "Mulk-nomans" (November 4th, 1805, when going down the Columbia River). On the return trip April 3rd, 1806, they said on reaching the lower end of Wappatoo Island, "The Indians call the river (meaning the river to the south of the islands, and also the Willamette River up to the falls at Oregon City) 'Multnomah,' from a nation of the same name residing near it on Wappatoo Island." Multnomah means "Down the River," and Willamette "Green Water." Wappatoo Island was "The most important spot * * * The chief wealth of this island consists of the numerous ponds in the interior abounding with the common arrowhead (Sagittaria sagittifolia, Sagittaria variabilis) to the root of which is attached a bulb growing beneath it in the mud. This bulb to which the Indians give the name of Wappatoo, is the great article of food and almost the staple article of commerce on the Columbia. It is never out of season; so that at all times of the year the valley is frequented by the neighboring Indians who came to gather it; it is collected chiefly by the women. * * * This plant is found through the whole extent of the valley in which we now are, but does not grow in the Columbia farther eastward.

"The nations which inhabit this fertile region are very numerous * * *. All these tribes who live somewhat lower on the river, and have an old village on Deer Island, may be considered as parts of the great Multnomah Nation which has its principal residence on Wappatoo Island, near the mouth of the large river which they give their name. * * * All the tribes in the neighborhood of Wappatoo Island we have considered as Multnomahs, not because they are in any degree subordinate to that nation, but as they all seem to regard the Multnomahs as the most powerful. There is no distinguishing chief, except the one at the head of the Multnomahs."

For several years, beginning in 1829, a deadly sickness prevailed among the Indians in the valley of the lower Columbia, west of The Dalles. Dr. McLoughlin believed that upwards of thirty thousand (about nine-tenths of all the Indians in that vicinity) died of measles, or fever and ague, which had never been known by them before or since. Some attributed it to the ploughing of the fields, which was done for the first time in that year. The Indians resorted to the "sweat bath"—their standard remedy, which was followed by a cold plunge, and a burial ceremony, until there were none left to perform that last sad rite.

"Cazenove, the first chief of the Chinook Nation," the Reverend Samuel Parker tell us in 1835, "was a great warrior, and before the desolating sickness, which commenced in the year 1829, could bring a thousand warriors into action. He is a man of talents, and his personal appearance is noble, and ought to represent a nature kind and generous; but such is his character, that his influence is retained among his people more by fear than by affection."

Paul Kane, the artist, tells us in 1846: "The Flat-Heads are divided into numerous tribes, each having its own peculiar locality, language, customs and manners. Those in the immediate vicinity of the fort are principally Chinooks and Klickitats, and are governed by a chief called Ca-sa-nov. Casanov is a man of advanced age, and resides principally at Fort Vancouver. I made a sketch (No. 8) of him while staying at the fort. Previous to 1829 Casanov was considered a powerful chief, and could lead into the field 1,000 men.

"His own immediate family, consisting of ten wives, four children, and eighteen slaves, were reduced in one year to one wife, one child, and two slaves.

"Casanov is a man of more than ordinary talent for an Indian, and he has maintained his great influence over his tribe chiefly by means of the superstitious dread in which they hold him. For many years, in the early period of his life, he kept a hired assassin to remove any obnoxious individual against whom he entertained personal enmity. This brave, whose occupation was no secret, went by the name of Casanov's Scoocoom, or the 'Evil Genius.' He finally fell in love with one of Casanov's wives, who eloped with him. Casanov vowed vengeance, but the pair for a long time eluded his search; until one day he met his wife in a canoe near the mouth of the Cowlitz River, and shot her on the spot, and at last procured also the assassination of the lover.

"A few years before my arrival at Fort Vancouver, Mr. Douglass, who was then in charge, heard from his office the report of a gun inside the gates. This being a breach of discipline he hurried out to inquire the cause of so unusual a circumstance, and found one of Casanov's slaves standing over the body of an Indian whom Casanov had just killed, * *

"Sacred as the Indians hold their burial places, Casanov himself, a short time after the latter occurrence, had his only son buried in the cemetery of the Fort. He died of consumption—a disease very common amongst all Indians, and after the conclusion of the ceremony, Casanov returned to his lodge, and the same evening attempted the life of the bereaved mother, who was the daughter of the great chief generally known as King Comcomly, so beautifully alluded to in Washington Irving's 'Astoria.' She was formerly the wife of a Mr. McDougall, who bought her from her father for, as it was supposed, the enormous price of ten articles of each description, guns, blankets, knives, hatchets, etc., then in Fort Astoria."

The Reverend Samuel Parker attended the funeral of Casanov's only son, "The heir to his chieftainship," who was given Christian burial at Fort Vancouver, Tuesday, February 2nd, 1836. Casanov "had the coffin made large for the purpose of putting in clothing, blankets and such other articles, as he supposed necessary for his son in the world to which he was gone." Dr. McLoughlin cared for Casanov and his household during the remaining years of their lives. The favorite walking stick, the one which Dr. McLoughlin almost always carried, was a "sword cane." The head of this sword, which is an excellent quality of steel, is elephant's tusk ivory, carved in the likeness of Casanov, no doubt when he was much younger than when Paul Kane sketched him in 1846. The "sword cane" was presented by Mrs. Josiah Myrick, a granddaughter of Dr. McLoughlin, to Mr. Frederick V. Holman, President of the Oregon Historical Society, and author of "Dr. John McLoughlin, the Father of Oregon."

Casanov, by Paul Kane

Mr. Holman kindly consented to permit the cane to be photographed for use in this publication.

Indian Beads and Mediums of Exchange. Gambling

The Indians east of the Cascade Range, who lived on plain and mountain top, regarded their horses most highly and all standards of value were measured by their ponies. Peu-peu-mox-mox, the great chief of the Walla Walla Indians, whose wealth in ponies was estimated at one hundred thousand dollars, saw the curly hair of a little nine months' old girl peeping out from behind a wagon cover just before dusk on a hot August day in the summer of 1853. George H. Himes,* her little brother, then a lad of ten years, was keeping watch while the men busied themselves with oxen and horses and his mother prepared the evening meal. Peu-peu-mox-mox was a stalwart man, richly dressed in fringed garments of buckskin, decorated with many ornaments, and highly colored bead work across his full chest. On his head was a large bonnet of eagle feathers. He came close to the wagon and looked intently at the child for several minutes then went away. The next morning hundreds of pinto ponies were grazing close by the camp. They had been driven up by the slaves of Chief Peu-peu-mox-mox, who came to buy the little red-haired girl. He offered ponies and ponies, and still more and more ponies. The family thought it a joke, but the old chief was serious and strode away with his company of attendants and exclaimed, "Ni-ka-tum-tum wake skoo-kum" (my heart is sick) because all of his wealth could not buy one red-headed baby girl.

Paul Kane, the artist, tells us that "Yellow-cum is the wealthiest man of his tribe. His property consists principally of slaves and ioquas, a small shell found at Cape Flattery, and only there, in great abundance. These shells are used as money and a great traffic is carried on among the tribes by means of them. They are obtained at the bottom of the sea, at a considerable depth, by means of a long pole stuck in a flat board about fifteen inches square. From this board a number of bone pieces project, which, when pressed down, enter the hollow ends of the shells, which seem to be attached to the bottom by their small ends. The shells stick on the pieces, and are thus brought to the surface. They are from an inch and a half to two inches in length, and are white, slender and hollow, and taper to a point, slightly curved and about the size of an ordinary pipe stem.† They are valuable in proportion to their length, and their value increases according to a fixed ratio, forty shells being the standard number to extend to a fathom's length; which number in that case is equal to a beaver skin; but if thirty-nine be enough to equal a fathom, it will be worth two beaver skins; if thirty-eight, three skins, and so on, increasing one beaver skin for every shell less than the standard number.

"The skin of a sea otter was worth twelve blankets, and two blankets were equal to a gun." A bushel of wheat was worth one dollar or one beaver skin and the Hudson's Bay Company required the Indians to give a pile of beaver skins laid out flat, one on top of the other, as high as the flint-lock gun which he wished to purchase. No doubt this accounts for the length of some of the guns. The Indians of the lower Columbia river were inveterate gamblers.

Type of flint-lock gun used by Hudson's Bay Company

---

*Mr. George H. Himes, of the Oregon Historical Society.
†The Nez Perce (pierced nose) Indians pierced the septum of the nose and wore two of these shells with the small ends out, one on each side of the nose, resembling a moustache.

APPENDIX "F"
Coinage of Gold into Beaver Money

On January 24, 1848, gold was discovered in California in the vicinity of Sutter's fort, near Sacramento, by two pioneers named James W. Marshall and Charles Bennett, who crossed the plains to Oregon in 1844. Both of these men were mechanics, who were

employed by Capt. John Sutter in 1847 to build a saw mill. On the day mentioned bright particles or pellets were found in the sand at the end of the mill race by Marshall and Bennett. The latter, having worked in the gold mines of Georgia about 1840, declared the pellets were gold. The first public announcement of the discovery was on March 15, 1848, in a San Francisco paper. The news reached the Willamette Valley in July following. Almost every able-bodied man that could provide an outfit left for the mines at once. Late in the fall thousands of dollars in gold dust were brought to Oregon City. There were three grades— valued at $12.00, $14.00, and $16.00 per ounce, depending on the cleanliness of the dust. This created dissatisfaction, as people were liable to be deceived unless gold scales were accessible. William H. Rector petitioned the Provisional Legislature, then in session, to pass a law providing for coinage. Such a law passed on February 16, 1849, and officers were elected to carry out its provisions. Prior to this date, however, the "Oregon Exchange Company," composed of eight well-known citizens, was organized, and put into circulation $58,500—$30,000 in Five Dollar pieces and $28,500 in Ten Dollar pieces, under the supervision of Mr. Rector. A hand rolling mill was built of scraps and old wagon tires by Thomas Powell. Hamilton Campbell engraved the Five Dollar die, and Victor M. Wallace the Ten Dollar die. On the obverse side of the Five Dollar die these words appear: "Oregon Exchange Company, 130 G. Native Gold. 5 D." On the reverse side, these initials: "K. M. T. A. W. R. C. S.," which stand for William K. Kilborne, Theophilus Magruder, James Taylor, George Abernethy, William H. Willson, William H. Rector,

John G. Campbell, Noyes Smith, members of the "Exchange Company." Under the initials there is a figure of a beaver, and below "T. O." standing for "Territory of Oregon," and "1849," to indicate the year of coinage. This description applies to the Five Dollar die only. The Ten Dollar is somewhat different, the obverse side being changed to indicate the larger denomination value, and on the reverse side the initials "A" and "W," standing for Abernethy and Willson, were omitted, and the initials below the Beaver transposed to "O. T." for "Oregon Territory."

While the end of the Provisional Government came when Governor Joseph Lane, by virtue of his appointment by President Polk, issued his proclamation on March 3, 1849, setting up the government of Oregon Territory according to the laws of the United States, yet the "Beaver Coinage" did not go out of circulation until about 1854, and then the larger portion went to the United States Mint in San Francisco, just established, because the bullion value of the coins — being pure gold—was from eight to ten per cent greater than the face value.

George H. Himes, Oregon Historical Society.

Chief Joseph, the Nez Perce

Chief Joseph or "Younger Joseph," has been called "The Red Napoleon." Colonel C. E. S. Wood and other historians have told of his bravery and skill in out-classing his pursuers in the War of 1877. General Miles and General Howard, who fought him, agree in saying that he possessed great skill as a military genius, and while it was their duty as officers to capture him and his followers, they respected him.

CHIEF JOSEPH, THE NEZ PERCE

Chief Joseph was every inch a man and it is a pity that civilized white men could not have found a better way of treating him.

Chief Joseph said: "Suppose a white man should come to me and say, 'Joseph, I like your horses and I want to buy them.' I say to him, 'No, my horses suit me; I will not sell them.' Then he goes to my neighbor and says to him, 'Joseph has some good horses. I want to buy them, but he refuses to sell.' My neighbor answers, 'Pay me the money and I will sell you Joseph's horses.' Then the white man turns to me and says, 'Joseph, I have bought your horses and you must let me have them.' If we sold our lands to the Government, that is the way they were bought."

Hear this stalwart man of the plain and the mountain top speak again: "I said in my heart, rather than have war I would give up my country. I would give up my father's grave. I would give up everything rather than have the blood of white men upon the hands of my people."

PURSE OF CHIEF JOSEPH

Presented to Samuel Hill by Chief Yellow Bull, June 20, 1905, at the unveiling of the monument erected by the Washington State University Historical Society, over the grave of Chief Joseph on the Colville Indian Reservation. On this occasion Mr. Hill was made honorary chief of the Nez Perce tribe and was named Wya-Tana-Toowa-Tykt, which translated, means "Necklace of Lightning." Chief Yellow Bull, now old and almost blind, wore the war bonnet and beaded paraphernalia of Chief Joseph. He rode around the "long-lodge" or potlatch tepee, astride Joseph's favorite horse, and delivered the following oration:

"When the Creator created us, he put us on this earth, and the flowers on this earth, and he takes us all in his arms and keeps us in peace and friendship, and our friendship and peace shall never fade, but it will shine forever. Our people love our old customs. I am very glad to see our white friends here attending this ceremony, and it seems like we all have the same sad feelings, and that would seem like it would wipe my tears. Joseph is dead; but his words are not dead; his words will live forever. This monument will stand—Joseph's words will stand as long as this monument. We (the red and white people) are both here, and the Great Spirit looks down on us both; and now if we are good and live right, like Joseph, we shall see him. I have finished."

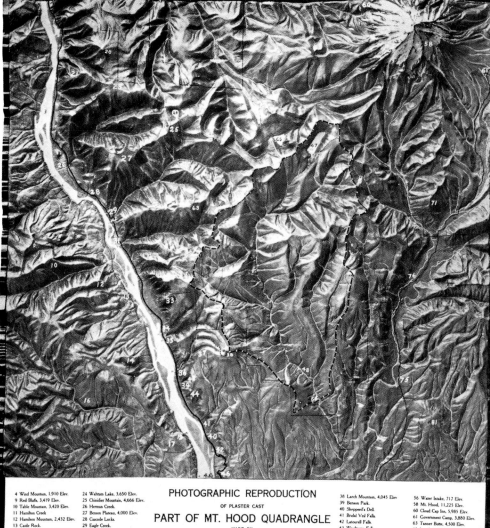

The Columbia River Highway and the Barlow Road are indicated by solid black lines. The dotted black line follows the top of the ridge that marks the divide and embraces Bull Run River, the source of Portland's water supply. Larch Mountain lifts its head four thousand and forty-five feet above the river, commanding a superb view of the entire surrounding country. Five great snow-capped peaks can be seen from the top. Easy foot and pony trails have been constructed all the way up to the summit. Beginning at Multnomah Falls a trail loops back and forth on the steep sides of the cliffs, and passes into a box canyon higher up, where there are many waterfalls.

This trail, constructed by "The Progressive Business Men's Club" of Portland, aided by Mr. S. Benson and his son Mr. Amos S. Benson, continues, and is met by another one which comes up from Wahkeena (Most Beautiful) Falls. It follows a babbling brook and a succession of musical waterfalls for a great part of the way, and so the trail continues through fern and wood to the craggy top of Nature's grandstand.

When God made the mountains and parted the range like a curtain, in order to permit this great river to pass through, almost at the level of the sea, He lifted up Larch Mountain to which the Children of Men might climb to look upon the wonders of His mighty work. "Be still and know that I am God; saith the Lord of Hosts."

When little Samuel, the nephew of the author, was about to ascend the slopes of Mount Rainier, he said to his mother: "If we go up in the clouds at Mount Rainier will we see God? * * * *Why won't we?*" We hope he will, for life is not life without seeing Him.

In the year A. D. 1915, great progress was made on the Pacific Coast of North America. No event was of greater importance than the construction of the Columbia River Highway in the State of Oregon. The last barrier between the "Inland Empire" and the Pacific Ocean has been removed. A broad thoroughfare almost

FOUR-COLOR REPRODUCTION OF PANORAMIC PAINTING BY FRED H. ROUTLEDGE OF PORTLAND, OREGON. AWARDED
FIRST PRIZE PANAMA-PACIFIC EXPOSITION, SAN FRANCISCO, CALIFORNIA. COPYRIGHT 1915, SAMUEL C. LANCASTER.

two hundred miles in length now passes through the two mountain ranges. All grades are easy, the maximum being five per cent. The curves are graceful; the shortest radius is one hundred feet, and there is always a good sight ahead. The road is everywhere twenty-four feet in width. Beautiful concrete bridges and strong

otection railings make it safe and comfortable. Multnomah County has expended $1,250,000.00 in paving this eat highway and other trunk roads leading to Portland. Crown Point can be reached in one hour, and the rge of the Columbia, in the heart of the Cascade range, in two hours from Portland.

(Continued from page 3)

The three Sams as he called them were himself, highway visionary and peace lover Sam Hill, and publisher of the *Oregon Journal* Sam Jackson. Simon Benson and John Yeon joined the struggle to convince Multnomah County citizens to put up millions in tax monies in 1913. The deluxe highway was completed by 1915. All while the First World War was ravaging Europe. No federal money was spent on building the Columbia Highway! This was a time when cars were a luxury to the ordinary person. Of course there was opposition, but also opportunity. For a complete detailed discussion, read the June, 1973 *Oregon Historical Quarterly*.

When the Columbia River Highway was offered to the world in June, 1916 during the Portland Rose Festival, the *Illustrated London News* called it "the King of Roads." It was "the best of all great highways in the world, glorified!" Teddy Roosevelt, who gave us our National Park system, agreed. A caravan of celebrities and politicians gathered at the Vista House at Crown Point for the dedication. Motion picture cameras whirred to capture and distribute the image. Precisely at 5 p.m., President Wilson touched an electric button in the White House "to unfurl the flag of freedom to the breezes."

Where did Sam Hill and Sam Lancaster get their inspiration for such a remarkable achievement? The utopian Hill took engineer Lancaster to Paris in 1908, as the American delegation to the First International Road Congress. The friends studied advancements in highway engineering and construction techniques. They traveled on famous roadways in France, Italy, Switzerland and Germany. It was a visit to the fabled Rhine River Valley, Lancaster writes, which caused Hill to imagine a beautiful highway in the Columbia River Gorge. Lancaster felt dubious at the time, but he would soon oversee and complete Hill's concept.

The two had collaborated on civic improvement projects in Washington State. They met in Seattle, and Hill recruited Lancaster as a consulting engineer with the Seattle Parks Department. He would work on the scenic boulevards surrounding Seattle, at Maryhill, and Goldendale. He was a lobbyist for the Mt. Rainier roadway. Both a dreamer and a doer, the eccentric millionaire Sam Hill created lasting grandiose public works besides the highway described and illustrated in this volume.

Across the river and inland from The Dalles, I see an extension of his vision known as Maryhill Museum. Three miles beyond it, he created a replica of Stonehenge to honor young soldiers from Klickitat County who were killed in the war. Hill also built the Peace Arch at Blaine on the Canadian border. Visit Maryhill Museum to marvel at Rodin sculptures, the furniture and jewels of Queen Marie of Rumania, chess sets, and Indian relics. This world-class museum sits out there in sand and sagebrush. No wonder Hill's biography is titled *Sam Hill: The Prince of Castle Nowhere*.

The shape of the land and the geology created by awesome natural forces—such as the Bretz floods—gave Hill and Lancaster their mission. Following through superbly, they absorbed the poetry and the ecology of the gorge. Mighty basalt bluffs, side canyons, fields of rare wildflowers, and panoramic vistas—all needed to be taken into account. Lancaster's task as he saw it was to find and enhance "beauty spots." The old road was designed to twist and turn, to contain loops and turnouts with a grade of no more than five percent. Italian stonemasons built signature stone railings into which "they sang their souls." Delicate pressed-concrete bridges elfinly show off unique spaces.

A heavy volume of traffic, trucks and all, was breaking down the old highway in the 1940s. Change began with the building of Bonneville Dam in 1938, after which Woody Guthrie came out to promote public power. Visiting Shepperd's Dell in autumn, with red and gold leaves falling, is a Zen moment from old Japan. At the western end of the highway, all waterfalls are treated specially. Their names and the scenic viewpoints are poetic—Latourell, Bridal Veil, Angel's Rest, Wahkeena, Multnomah (the 2nd highest waterfall in the U.S.), Oneonta (mossy green cleft with a waterfall at the back), Horsetail, St. Peter's Dome.

Today the poetic trance lasts until the original Columbia Highway is superseded by I-84 near Dodson. Because the old roadway parallels the river-level freeway, legislation was needed to protect it. America's first grand gesture to the automobile might have been dismantled one stone at a time. Instead, Senator Hatfield and others created the Columbia River Gorge National Scenic Area in 1986. The dream is hopefully preserved forever.

Just west of the town of Hood River, the Mitchell Point Tunnel with its five stone windows was sheared off when I-84 was built in the 1960s. Hill and Lancaster were trying to surpass a Swiss three-windowed model (pgs. 120-24). Sam Hill used to boast: "Talk about Switzerland. There are thirty Switzerlands in Oregon." After Hood River, one returns to the old highway taking the Rowena Loop. The state of Oregon has restored most of the Columbia Highway to varied modes of travel. The Mosier Twin Tunnels can be hiked or biked. Journeying on Lancaster's road gives a lesson in engineering and esthetics. The truth is that technology and nature can be compatible. Inspiration comes from natural beauty before man puts his mark or scar upon the land.

WALT CURTIS

THE GREAT ROCK—CROWN POINT—COLUMBIA RIVER HIGHWAY.
This rock stands 725 feet above the mile wide river. The Columbia River Highway encircles the top of it. A reinforced concrete side-walk and railing extend around the outer edge of the roadway and every 20 feet there is a lamp post with its electrolier. The Vista House, a pioneer memorial, occupies the center of the circle. (See page 17.) Compare the bulk of the great rock with the Union Pacific Passenger Train.

LOOKING EAST FROM SHEPPERD'S DELL—COLUMBIA RIVER HIGHWAY.

This great pillar of basalt forms the east gateway to Shepperd's Dell. It was necessary to cut under the side of this rock in order to secure the full width of roadway and permit a good sight ahead. It is one of the many attractive features in Shepperd's Dell. The workmen called it "a half tunnel."

SAINT PETER'S DOME—COLUMBIA RIVER HIGHWAY.

This mighty monolith is one of several, that stand like sentinels in the Gorge of the Columbia. The clouds play "hide and seek" around their heads, and the eagles make their nests among the crags. Every one who drives over the broad highway passes near the base of these towers of strength, that have withstood the centuries.

ASTORIA COLUMN

VENDOME COLUMN

The Astoria monument on the crest of Coxcomb Hill, Astoria, Oregon, was conceived by Ralph Budd, president of the Great Northern Railway. He interested Vincent Astor, the grandson of John Jacob Astor, founder of Astoria, and gave every possible assistance in maturing and executing the plans.

The observation platform is seven hundred and fifty feet above the river, overlooking the Pacific ocean and all of the country which figured in the beginnings of the historical record of the Pacific Northwest.

A MAGNIFICENT VIEW POINT—COLUMBIA RIVER HIGHWAY.

This curving road, on the Oregon side of the Columbia, winds around the steep sides of the mountain on easy grades, the maximum being five percent. There is always a good sight ahead and everywhere the traveler is protected from danger by strong walls of stone and concrete.

SEASIDE—THE END OF THE LEWIS AND CLARK TRAIL.

The Columbia River Highway parallels the great Continental River which Lewis and Clark explored in 1805-6, from the Dalles in eastern Oregon, through the Cascade Mountains and the Coast Range to Astoria and Seaside.

The Courage of Samuel Lancaster

BY

MARGURITE NORRIS DAVIS

*It is hoped that this reprint from St. Nicholas Magazine, of March, 1924, may
cheer some shut-in friend who may be discouraged. Dark days come to all of us.
Despair takes hold of our heart-strings and we pray that death may soon end all.
Through faith in God we are able to conquer.*

SAMUEL CHRISTOPHER
LANCASTER

Thirty-six years ago, in a little town in western Tennessee, a young man had just learned that he would probably never walk again.

His name was Samuel C. Lancaster, known perhaps the world over as the engineer who built the Columbia River Highway, one of the most beautiful mountain drives on the face of the globe. It is the same indomitable courage which raised him from helpless invalidism to physical power that has enabled him to perform works which bequeath worthy things to coming generations.

Close to Mr. Lancaster's heart has always lain the desire to bring happiness to mankind, and to develop in others the same love for the beautiful in nature which has even been his.

"My love for the beautiful is inherited from my mother," he told me one day, as we drove slowly along the Loops of Latourell, where the Columbia River Highway parallels itself five times, winding in and out, between the flowering shrubs and ferns, beneath great, stately trees.

"When I made my preliminary survey here and found myself standing waist-deep in the ferns, I remembered my mother's long-ago warning, 'Oh, Samuel, do be careful of my Boston fern!'

"And I then pledged myself that none of this wild beauty should be marred where it could be prevented. The highway was so built that not one tree was felled, not one fern was crushed, unnecessarily."

No thoughtful person, passing along this road, can but be impressed with the fact that it took not only superior technical knowledge to build it, but also physical prowess to do the original surveying and the subsequent supervising of road-building. With very little exception, the thoroughfare was cut through unbroken area. It took a man of strength and courage to plunge through the dense underbrush and blaze a trail over mountain and through forest. At times, Lancaster and his men dangled like spiders on a web as they let themselves down, hand over hand, by means of ropes hung over the edge of a cliff. And yet this strong, muscular man was once as helpless as a baby—more so, because an infant can grasp, with almost unbelievable power, a finger placed in its palm, while there were eighteen months in Lancaster's life when he could not even move his fingers!

"I would never have told any one my story," Mr. Lancaster said to me, "were it not for the boy in *St. Nicholas*, and what his story did for me. Had I never heard of him, I should never have climbed mountains; I should never have had a part in building this highway, with its ever-changing landscape; nor should I now be engaged in preserving, for all ages, some of the most beautiful spots in the world."

Samuel Christopher Lancaster was born in 1865, at Magnolia, Mississippi, near New Orleans, but moved with his parents to Jackson, Tennessee, when a small boy. In the panic of 1873, his father's money was swept away, and, as the eldest of five children, it was necessary for him to assume a great deal of responsibility. He was able to finish the first year of college, and then continued his engineering studies under the guidance of the chief engineer of the southern lines of the Illinois Central Railroad.

It was later that a very serious illness, infantile paralysis, was brought on by a combination of malaria, exposure and overwork. While the doctors held out no hope of his recovery, through the tender nursing of Samuel's mother, and her faith and that of the girl who later became his wife, he was brought back to health and strength again. But before that time arrived, young Lancaster had to fight—and win—his courageous battle.

For eighteen months, the young engineer was paralyzed, with the exception of his head, which he was able to move. His limbs, fingers, and toes were crippled in such a way that they were bent entirely out of shape, and in spite of his most earnest efforts, he found himself unable to make any progress toward recovering the use of them, until gradually the tendons throughout his body had begun to harden.

But Samuel Lancaster made up his mind that in some way he was going to move his limbs again. Beginning with his hands, he concentrated every ounce of his willpower toward moving the middle finger of one of them. He will always remember it as one of the hardest tasks ever set before him. It was a battle royal for him, but he came out victorious.

At about this time his mother read him a true story, appearing in *St. Nicholas*, about a boy who had been crippled to the same extent as he. Unable to move hands or feet, this lad had learned to paint pictures, with a paintbrush held between his teeth, thus earning a livelihood.

Here was a definite idea, something tangible upon which to work. Soon after that, by almost super-human effort, Samuel got a pencil between his teeth; and, by throwing his head forward, found he could touch a piece of paper with the pencil. However, he soon discovered that he did not have the proper hold on the pencil, and it took him several days to discover that, by placing it lengthwise in his mouth, so that the teeth front and back had a chance to grip hard, he could make a steady mark! In a few weeks he could write quite a legible "hand," and took charge of his own correspondence with sweetheart and friends. His courage had carried him through.

Lancaster now made up his mind that he was going to stand alone, in spite of the fact that hitherto, when members of his family had lifted him to his feet, he had crumbled up like a punctured balloon, even as they strove to hold him upright. In his mind grew a picture of a frame that could be built and which would keep him upright, once he was placed in it. His family felt that such a contrivance was out of the question, so he quietly drew the plan he had in mind, and gave it to a carpenter. Laboriously drawn though this plan had been, with pencil held between his teeth, its measurements were accurate. The wooden frame, with rollers, was made without difficulty, and this the invalid used for some time.

How carefully Mr. Lancaster had designed this contrivance is shown by his description of how exactly it fitted his needs. He tells us that, when strapped into the frame, he could neither fall nor slip out of it. When they put him into his "carriage," there he remained, until released! Wisdom had warned him that he must not overtax his strength, so he began by using the frame for only three minutes at a time, increasing the period each day by this amount. It did not take him long to discover that, by great effort, his toes could be pushed against the floor, which moved the frame backward. And in this manner he moved himself about for the next few months!

One day, when the frame had been strapped on as usual, he announced that he was going to stand alone. By concentrating every ounce of will-power, he did raise his arms from their supports, place his feet on the floor, and stand, unaided. His sister's cry of joy distracted his attention, breaking the spell, and, missing his usual support, he fell, slipping through the straps. As can be imagined, this accident was extremely painful; but the young engineer soon learned that it was also very fortunate. His weight crushing upon his toes, had bent the crippled tendons from their unnatural position, and, though it had meant agony to him, Mr. Lancaster knew that the same process was necessary throughout his entire body; the tendons must be loosened by force, and then kept in place and in an active state by exercise and massage. In spite of the excruciating pain, he kept steadily at it, with about three years from the time he was first taken ill, he had recovered with the

exception of some of the muscles of his feet. However, he did not wait long before going back to work. He was still on crutches, with crippled feet and fingers, when he went after an engineering job and obtained it.

It was in a frame similar to this, that Samuel Lancaster learned to walk again.

This frame and others like it have been made under Mr. Lancaster's direction for disabled boys and girls who have been given new faith and hope because of his encouragement.